YO-BRU-644

An Interpersonal Approach to
Classroom Management

Strategies for Improving Student Engagement

Heather A. Davis | Jessica J. Summers
Lauren M. Miller

A Joint Publication

CORWIN
A SAGE Company

FOR INFORMATION:

Corwin

A SAGE Company

2455 Teller Road

Thousand Oaks, California 91320

(800) 233-9936

www.corwin.com

SAGE Publications Ltd.

1 Oliver's Yard

55 City Road

London EC1Y 1SP

United Kingdom

SAGE Publications India Pvt. Ltd.

B 1/I 1 Mohan Cooperative Industrial Area

Mathura Road, New Delhi 110 044

India

SAGE Asia-Pacific Pte. Ltd.

3 Church Street

#10-04 Samsung Hub

Singapore 049483

Acquisitions Editor: Jessica Allan

Associate Editors: Allison Scott and Julie Nemer

Editorial Assistant: Lisa Whitney

Production Editors: Amy Schroller and Melanie Birdsall

Copy Editor: Dawn Moews

Typesetter: C&M Digitals (P) Ltd.

Proofreader: Tracy Villano

Indexer: Joan Shapiro

Cover Designer: Edgar Abarca

Permissions Editor: Karen Ehrmann

Printed in the United States of America

Library of Congress Cataloging-in-Publication Data

Davis, Heather A.

An interpersonal approach to classroom management: Strategies for improving student engagement/Heather A. Davis, Jessica J. Summers, Lauren M. Miller.

A Joint Publication With APA Division 15: Educational Psychology

p. cm.—(Classroom insights from educational psychology) Includes bibliographical references and index.

ISBN 978-1-4129-8673-1 (pbk. : alk. paper)

1. Classroom management. 2. Teacher-student relationships. 3. Educational psychology.
I. Summers, Jessica J. II. Miller, Lauren M. III. Title.

LB3013.D378 2012
371.102'4–dc23   2012020445

This book is printed on acid-free paper.

Certified Chain of Custody
Promoting Sustainable Forestry
www.sfiprogram.org
SFI-01268

SFI label applies to text stock

12 13 14 15 16 10 9 8 7 6 5 4 3 2 1

An Interpersonal Approach to
Classroom Management

Classroom Insights from Educational Psychology Series

A Developmental Approach to
Educating Young Children
Denise H. Daniels and Patricia K. Clarkson

Transforming Teaching and Learning
Through Data-Driven Decision Making
Ellen B. Mandinach and Sharnell S. Jackson

An Interpersonal Approach to
Classroom Management: Strategies
for Improving Student Engagement
*Heather A. Davis, Jessica J. Summers,
and Lauren M. Miller*

Contents

Preface

Classroom learning environments are constantly changing—with each new group of students, with the addition of one or two new students, with the rhythm of the school year, and with changes in curriculum. Often, our goal is to anticipate these changes by trying to organize our classrooms to avoid disruption, establishing rules and procedures, and consistently following through. As teachers, we often think that if we are in control, then we will maximize student on-task behavior and their learning, right?

But what if our primary focus was on managing *relationships* rather than on managing individual students? What does it mean to manage classroom relationships for learning? For us, the answer is complex. It involves not only recognizing the variety of needs and goals each student brings to our classroom, but also developing authentic relationships with our students that are built around the desire to learn and grow together.

With so many individual differences and so much content to cover, it may feel like an impossible task to create a classroom culture where everyone has "bought in" to the learning objectives and each member shares in the responsibility to meet those objectives. However, many teachers achieve this culture in some of the most difficult teaching situations. It requires a willingness to reconsider why our current approaches to classroom management may not bring about the outcomes we want or are not working well for students. And it requires a willingness to consider what we might be missing or misunderstanding when we attempt to manage students without first understanding and managing relationships.

Managing relationships to enhance student learning requires us to adopt a developmental perspective on children and adolescents' interactions and behaviors, to consider not only the kinds of behaviors we'd like to see them exhibit *now* but also in the future. And managing relationships can require us to move out of our cultural comfort zones and recognize that other families, classrooms, and communities interact in ways that feel foreign to us.

Our purpose in writing this book is to share with teachers what it means to manage classroom relationships for learning and how to think about each dimension of our instruction in a way that optimizes three interconnected types of student engagement: relational, cognitive, and behavioral. In this book, we describe an integrative, relational approach to understanding *classroom management.* We draw from the work of educational psychologists who largely argue that disruptive student behavior, inattention, and lower performance occur when students are not actively engaged by the curriculum. We draw from the work of social developmental psychologists to examine how children think about their relationships in qualitatively different ways and how relational conflict (among students and with teachers) occurs as children learn to navigate increasingly multifaceted and complex relationships. And we draw from the work of sociocultural researchers who remind us that our identity as part of a "clan" affects the way we interact with each other and the curriculum, providing us frames of reference for interpreting events and skillsets for interacting with each other.

Heather

My interest in this book project grew out of my research in studying students' and teachers' understandings of their relationships with each other, and, in particular, a three-year collaboration with a district that was so committed to developing optimal relationships for all of the students in their district that they embarked on a wide-scale reform of their high schools. In interviews with teachers, I listened as teachers described with joy the successes they perceived in their abilities to connect with students, and then, with sorrow, the children they felt remained estranged despite their best efforts. I listened as students described teachers who were "really nice but I didn't learn much from them," classrooms where the culture prohibited being them from being "real," and schools where they knew every teacher cared about them. I learned that most teachers developed their relationship and management skills on the job and that those who were successful at connecting with kids credited it to their mentors: their own exemplary teachers, administrators, and colleagues. I learned that this makes for patchy knowledge—with only some teachers lucky enough to experience this kind of support. Today, as a teacher educator, I try to integrate knowledge and skills about relationships and management into my own courses in learning theory and child development. But I have also learned over the past 10 years that as we pack our teacher education curriculums with courses in academic content, courses in classroom management become optional. I wanted us to create a book that would bridge theory on teacher and peer relationships with actual tools that could be used to improve classroom climate and relationship quality.

Jessica

My interest in this book was inspired by Heather's strong commitment to the development of teacher-student relationships and my own interest in students' motivation and social interactions in the classroom. Specifically, most of my research has focused on students' motivation in collaborative/cooperative learning groups, asking such questions as, "Do students in groups influence each other's motivation for learning?", "Do feelings of classroom community affect their motivation to learn?", and "Do different types of group learning reduce student incivility in the classroom?" Although most of my findings are mixed, one consistency has been that teachers need to use interactive learning in very strategic ways if they are going to motivate their students to listen and learn, particularly as they try to build positive relationships in their classrooms.

Lauren

My interest in this project stemmed directly from my experiences as an elementary school teacher. While the importance of classroom management was emphasized throughout my traditional teacher preparation program, deliberate instruction in management theory and methodology was absent from my training until I began my student teaching program. And even then, most of my peers and I learned management techniques from our mentor teachers, which meant we were exposed to only *one* approach by *one* individual. In my own experience, the first few years of my teaching career started when I developed a management style, and even then it was mostly through a system of trial and error. It was my hope that we could create a text that could be used by teachers at all experience levels, from teacher education students in their earliest field experiences to seasoned educators searching for an alternative approach to management. I hope that this text prompts educators to reflect on the relationships they cultivate in their classrooms and to think in new ways about management.

This book was written in order to share our ideas about what it means to take a *relational* perspective on classroom management. It presents our unique perspectives and approaches to designing classrooms that consider, holistically, the social-developmental needs of children and adolescents, and creating teacher and peer relationships that provide optimal environments for motivation and learning. Although we recognize that creating optimal classrooms for learning is far easier when teachers have the support of their colleagues and administrators, we focus on identifying strategies that can empower teachers to transform their classrooms even without this support.

This work stands on the shoulders of many other researchers across the fields of classroom management, motivation theory, social and emotional development, culturally relevant pedagogy, and teachers and mentors we have worked with throughout our careers. At the end of each chapter, we highlight accessible readings, websites, and reviews of literature that can support future inquiry. Scholar James Wertsch (1991) described how the people we interact with can become the "voices in our mind," guiding individual thoughts and behaviors. In this way, our thinking was shaped by assumptions or prominent voices cited at the end of this text:

1. Children and adolescents will *thrive* academically in classrooms where they feel connected to their teacher

and their peers (Ryan, Connell, & Deci, 1985; Connell & Wellborn, 1991).

2. All classroom relationships are reciprocal, but teachers are leaders in their classrooms and possess the authority and power to shape the climate and quality of their relationships *with* and *among* their students (Hartup, 1989). ·

3. Opportunities for learning and development occur when teachers and students reflect openly on the quality of their relationships as well as on the culture and climate of the classroom. We invite you to adapt and photocopy any of the exercises in this text to use with your students.

This book also was designed to provide a gap in texts and professional development materials in teacher education in several ways:

1. By making explicit theoretical connections between the research and practice. We explicitly connect research on teachers' beliefs, student motivation, and the psychology of emotions and relationships with findings about the teachers' decision making on managing students' academic behavior and interacting in their classrooms.

2. By examining these theory-research-practice connections from our perspectives as classroom teachers, as researchers who listen to children and adolescents talk about their relationships and who study relationship dynamics, and as university-based teacher educators who empathize with the dearth of coursework and support available in many teacher preparation curriculums.

3. By offering tools for reflection, observation, and data collection (from students), we provide pathways for teachers to translate the ideas in this book into realities in their classrooms. We believe these activities can be

revisited each summer as you plan to greet a new class and also throughout the year as you identify dimensions of the climate or specific relationships that you desire to improve. We designed this book to be more than simply a discussion of how to improve classroom relationships. Instead, we view this text as an interactive workbook, designed to help you think through (sometimes inconspicuous) elements of instructional design.

We have structured the book in three parts. In Part I, Management as a Function of Student Engagement, we offer the perspective of educational psychologists on classroom management. Specifically, we define what it means for students to be engaged in the learning process, we offer an overview of basic tenets of motivation theory, and we outline the ways in which classroom structures contribute to student engagement. From an educational psychologist's perspective, classroom disruptions and relational conflict can be largely viewed as a function of poor student engagement. We offer tools and strategies for teachers to use in reflecting on their current beliefs and pedagogy and assessing how their students' view their classroom and school.

In Part II, Management as a Function of Classroom Relationships, we draw from the social-developmental literature on teacher-student and peer relationships to understand the nature of relational engagement. From this perspective, classroom disruptions and relational conflicts may be a function of problems with teacher or peer relationships. We devote much of this section to helping teachers reflect on their beliefs about teacher and peer relationships, their role in helping students develop into autonomous learners, and their ability to be in sync with diverse learners. We offer tools and strategies for modeling and caring about each other, learning in our relationships with students, and helping students learn to connect in meaningful ways with each other.

In Part III, Management as a Function of Teacher Self-Regulation, we attempt to empower teachers in their capacity to anticipate issues with student engagement. We review the tenets of self-regulation theory and apply these tenets—planning, instruction, interaction, assessment, and documentation—to teachers' classroom practices. From this perspective, classroom disruptions and relational conflict may be viewed as a function of breakdowns in the self-regulatory cycle. We offer strategies for systematically reflecting on dimensions of the classroom, our interactions with students, and for caring for ourselves so that we may sustain relationships with our students.

Acknowledgments

I would like to acknowledge the invaluable contributions of former Ohio State students: Carey E. Andrzejewski, Barbara Barta, Ann Bischoff, Paige Bruening, Yesim Capa, Mei-Lin Chang, Heather Dawson, Tony Durr, DeLeon Gray, Romena Holbert, Jennifer Kaschner, Steve Kucinksi, Melissa Newberry, Ryan R. Poirier, Gonul Sakiz, Sarah Kozel Silverman, Evan T. Straub, Elif Yetkin, and all of the students who enrolled in my Social Psychology in the Classroom course. I would also like to acknowledge my colleagues Paul Schutz, Dorene Ross, Anita Woolfolk Hoy, Lynley Anderman, Jessica DeCuir Gunby, Marc Grimmett, and the series editor, Deb Meyer. It is hard to measure how conversations during research team meetings, advising, and over cups of coffee contributed to this text and to my ongoing thinking about teacher-student relationship quality. I would also like to acknowledge the invaluable contributions of the teachers at Madison County Middle School, the ninth-grade teachers at Westerville North and Central High Schools, and Project Enlightenment (http://www.project enlightenment.wcpss.net/) educational consultants Edla Prevette and Caroline Tatum Carter.

—Heather A. Davis

I would like to acknowledge Heather for inviting me to be a part of this project. There is nothing I like better about my job than collaborating with people who care about education the way she does. I would like to acknowledge all of my former graduate students who helped make me a better researcher and teacher: Keith Ciani, Matt Easter, Diley Hernandez, Denise Kay, Gerard Robertson, Kelly Rodgers, Hale Thomas-Hillburn, and Linda Shealy. I would also like to acknowledge my colleagues and mentors: Sheri Bauman, David Bergin, Marilla Svinicki, and Jeannine Turner. Thank you for your guidance, support, and collaborative efforts over the years.

—*Jessica J. Summers*

I would like to acknowledge Heather for her time and support as an adviser and mentor. This project has changed the way I think about relationships at school and in my classroom; I know I am a better teacher, mentor, and colleague because of our work together. I also would like to acknowledge colleagues Dr. Alan Reiman, Melanie Smith, and Erin Horne of North Carolina State University. The instruction I received from each of you taught me so much about teacher support and professional development. I am a more reflective colleague and mentor because of each of you. I would like to acknowledge Jan Riggsbee, Lisa Carboni, and Kristen Stephens of Duke University. You each molded me into a teacher. From you I learned to care about and care for each of my students' individual needs. Finally, I would like to acknowledge my students, former, past, and present, who challenge, stimulate, and reward me each and every day.

—*Lauren M. Miller*

PUBLISHER'S ACKNOWLEDGMENTS

Corwin gratefully acknowledges the contributions of the following reviewers:

Sherry L. Annee
High School Science Teacher
Brebeuf Jesuit Preparatory School
Indianapolis, IN

Julie Duford
Fifth-Grade Teacher
Polson Middle School
Polson, MT

Hope Edlin
Teacher
Bethel Elementary School
Simpsonville, SC

Nancy L. Foote, NBCT
Middle School Teacher, Arizona Master Teacher
Higley Unified School District
Gilbert, AZ

Maria Mesires
Seventh-Grade Life Science Teacher
Case Middle School
Watertown, NY

Mary Reeve
Director, Special Education
Gallup McKinley County Schools
Gallup, NM

About the Authors

 **Dr. Heather A. Davis** is an Associate Professor in the Department of Curriculum, Instruction, and Counselor Education at North Carolina State University. Trained as an educational psychologist, her teaching interests surround helping preservice and practicing teachers use theories of development to meet their students' needs. For the last ten years, she has worked collaboratively with school districts throughout Georgia, Ohio, and North Carolina to understand the nature of teacher-student relationships and what it means to create schools that fully engage students in the learning process. Visit her at http://www4.ncsu.edu/~hadavis2/index.html.

 **Dr. Jessica J. Summers** is an Assistant Professor in the Department of Teaching, Learning and Sociocultural Studies at the University of Arizona. She previously served on the faculty of the University of Missouri–Columbia. Also trained as an educational psychologist, Dr. Summers's scholarship focuses on understanding the role of motivation and social relationships in learning and achievement, specifically how social context (as both processes and phenomena) affects students' motivation to learn, and how this contributes to students' overall success as learners. She currently serves on the editorial boards of *Contemporary Educational*

Psychology, the *Elementary School Journal,* the *Journal of Experimental Education,* and the *American Educational Research Journal.*

 **Lauren M. Miller** is a nationally board certified first-grade teacher at Durham Academy in Durham, North Carolina. She holds a master's degree in developmental supervision from the Department of Curriculum, Instruction, and Counselor Education at North Carolina State University. She has taught at public and private elementary schools in Durham, North Carolina; has supervised student teachers; and has conducted research on effective models for training supervisors and for teacher professional development.

Introduction

What Are Your Implicit Theories of Classroom Management?

OBSERVING STUDENT ENGAGEMENT

Lauren

One semester I supervised two women, both undergraduates in the same teacher education program, who were placed for student teaching in two very different classrooms. Alice was working in an upper-elementary classroom at a socioeconomically and racially diverse magnet school. The students in her classroom regularly engaged in conflict. Their verbal arguments and physical altercations were often related to racial or cultural differences between students. Alice took a relational approach to classroom management in which she sought to understand the causes of student conflict, connect those causes to student needs, and empower students to solve their disagreements independently. She encouraged her students to take ownership of their actions, to take each other's perspectives, and to appreciate both their differences and similarities.

Kim was also teaching in an upper elementary classroom at a socio-economically and racially diverse traditional school. The students in her classroom were quiet, obedient, and nearly always agreeable. Kim took a **traditional management approach** to classroom management; she sought to control negative behavior through verbal feedback and through a system of rewards and consequences. She expected students to do what they were told and took a position as the sole leader responsible for running the classroom.

The different approaches these two teachers took to management of student behavior in their classrooms transferred to their expectations and goals for their students. In a reflection about her experiences, Alice wrote about how her classroom code of conduct and her explicit social modeling would help her students grow into adults who were caring, capable of leadership, and who would be able to reconcile differences. Kim wrote about a realization that she needed to be consistent about providing specific and neutral verbal feedback to students who were misbehaving. She believed that providing this type of feedback would help her students learn to meet her expectations, to understand the rationale behind her expectations, and to understand right from wrong.

What types of thoughts and behaviors is each teacher encouraging in her students? If our goals for students are to develop critical thinking, problem solving, and leadership skills, which teacher fosters growth in those areas in her classroom?

CLASSROOM MANAGEMENT IN TODAY'S CLASSROOMS

Most states have adopted professional teaching standards that claim effective teachers help students develop critical thinking, problem solving, and leadership skills. This would include encouraging students to ask questions, develop innovative ideas, communicate their needs and collaborate with their peers, especially when their peers are from different cultures and backgrounds. What classroom management strategies are going to help us meet these goals in addition to sustaining the kind of engagement students need for meeting performance standards on academic indicators? While across content areas our instructional paradigms have shifted toward implementing methods that provide for student meaning making, many of our management practices in schools have not. Look at the statements below. Which ones best reflect your current views on your students' abilities to regulate their own academic and social behavior?

> Too much of students' time is spent on guidance and social activities at the expense of academic preparation.
>
> Students can be trusted to work together without supervision.
>
> Being friendly with students often leads them to become too familiar.
>
> It is important to try to understand the reasons for student misbehavior.

Where do these beliefs come from and what impact do they have on our classroom management decisions and ultimately on student learning and behavior? In 1976, Dan Lortie coined the term *apprenticeship of observation* to describe the phenomenon that most teachers teach using methods that are similar to those they observed used by their own teachers: "Teaching is unusual in that those who decide to enter it have had exceptional opportunity to observe members of the occupation at work; unlike most occupations today, the activities of teachers are not shielded from youngsters" (2002, p. 65). Lortie contends that many of the beliefs we hold as teachers about teaching and classroom originate from personal experiences as students. Most teachers never had a course or any guided practice in classroom management; instead we picked up management techniques spuriously from our colleagues or through our own trial and error. Whereas many of these beliefs may have been challenged in our teacher education programs or by reforms made to national and state standards, our intuitions about classroom management often remain unquestioned. We begin this text with an exploration of the underlying beliefs about classroom **discipline** that guide our planning and interactions with students.

TEACHERS' BELIEFS ABOUT DISCIPLINE

Our beliefs exist on many levels from global to personal and serve as overarching frameworks for how we understand and engage with the world. Our beliefs can be thought of as the guiding principles that we hold to be true and that serve as lenses through which we understand what happens in our classrooms. Fundamentally, our beliefs as teachers shape our professional practice guiding the everyday decisions we make about what and how to teach.

For over 40 years, scholars have examined the kinds of beliefs teachers hold about discipline and classroom management. In the 1960s, Willower, Eidell, and Hoy developed a survey to explore teachers' beliefs about discipline along two dimensions: custodial and caregiver. Teachers exemplifying a **custodial management orientation** tend to be concerned with controlling the classroom setting and maintaining a sense of order. Several studies suggest teachers who score high on the custodial dimension tend to feel pessimistic about teaching and are more likely to use punishment to control students' behavior. They are often worried about administering consequences equally for all students and tend not to be concerned with trying to understand the reasons that underlie student (mis)behavior. In contrast, teachers who score high on the caregiver orientation tend to hold more humanistic perspectives and view students as capable of learning to self-regulate their own relationships and behavior. These teachers view school as an educational community in which students learn through both cooperative and conflicted interactions with themselves and their peers. The focus is on helping students to develop their ability to exert self-control.

> Where do you see custodial and humanistic beliefs enacted in Alice's and Kim's teaching?

Beliefs about management can be enacted in the form of different orientations toward discipline (Glickman & Tamashiro, 1980; Wolfgang, 1999). For example, teachers who endorse predominantly custodial views of management often approach classroom discipline from a *rules-consequences* perspective. They view good behavior as the result of learning by experiencing consequences (rewards and punishments). This approach is often called an *interventionist* approach because teachers view themselves as responsible for deciding what behavior is needed for the classroom to run smoothly. They then assertively teach, monitor, and provide consequences as appropriate. Historically, the most common approach to classroom management had been some form of behavior modification. Indeed, many of the popular classroom management programs (i e , assertive discipline; posi tive behavior support) hail from a custodial/interventionist philosophy. For this reason, custodial/interventionist models reflect the traditional form of classroom management. Yet as we shift toward more innovative teaching methods that require students to work collaboratively, regulate their own behavior, and problem solve, many scholars question the appropriateness of these management techniques:

> Rules, consequences, rewards seem to be the mainstay of most teacher repertoires for student discipline. What is the source of this approach? How useful is it in an era of active learning curriculum and an emphasis on higher level thinking skills? (Frieberg, 1999a, p. 5)

Teachers with blended views of classroom management— that is, who endorse both custodial and humanistic, may approach discipline issues with *confronting-contracting* strategies. They view student (mis)behavior as a reflection of a student's inability to manage his or her own internal needs in the face of the external demands of classroom life. These teachers are sometimes called *interactionist* because they view themselves as serving a socializing role, helping students to understand and conform to a set of external standards (i.e., classroom tasks and rules). The goal of a confronting-contracting approach is to help the student identify and understand the purpose of each external standard and to develop the social

and academic skills necessary to be successful in the classroom setting.

Finally, teachers who endorse a predominantly **humanistic management orientation** often approach classroom discipline with a *relationship-listening orientation*. They tend to view
discipline problems in the classroom as representing a student's struggle to balance his or her own individual needs
with the needs of the class and the curriculum. These teachers
are often called *noninterventionists* because the goal of their
approach to discipline is to first listen to and understand what
need the student is trying to meet in a way that conflicts with
the needs of the teacher and the class. Then, the teacher
attempts to help students understand the needs of the teacher
and the class and learn to coordinate their needs with the
needs of the class. Because students' needs vary, noninterventionist teachers stress the importance of building relationships
with and between their students. Contemporary management
models (i.e., Conscious Discipline, Joyful Classroom, Consistency
Management, and Cooperative Discipline) that have developed
reflecting a caregiving and noninterventionist model are often
called *relationship models* or *community-based models*.

> What do you think are Alice's and Kim's
> orientations toward classroom discipline?

Figure 0.1 compares the basic tenets of traditional models
of classroom management with relationship-based models.
Traditional and **relationship-based management approaches**
of classroom management fundamentally differ in terms of
teachers' beliefs about control (i.e., Who can I control? Who
should be the leader in the classroom?), teachers' beliefs about
the source and direction of behavioral change (i.e., Who and
what should change when there is a problem in the classroom?), and teachers' beliefs about the meaning of conflict
(i.e., Does conflict reflect defiance or misunderstanding?). It is

important to note that classroom management systems that are based on rewards and consequences will, in the short term, result in declines in discipline referrals but also tend to result in more competitive climates in schools and classrooms. Moreover, teachers must have a plan in place for how to eventually wean students off those incentives. Classroom management plans based on relationship and community models not only result in fewer discipline referrals but also result in more

Figure 0.1 Comparing Traditional Views of Classroom Management With Relational Views of Classroom Management

Traditional Management Approaches

Teachers believe they can make children behave.

The teacher is the sole leader and takes responsibility for all paperwork and organization.

Students are allowed limited responsibilities with a few students serving as a teacher's helper.

Classroom rules govern the teacher's and the students' behavior.

Consequences are fixed for all students.

Management is a form of oversight

Teachers avoid conflicts by using rewards (bribes), consequences (threats), and manipulation.

Rewards are mostly extrinsic.

Discipline comes from the teacher.

Relationship-Based Management Approaches

Teachers understand the only person they can change is themselves.

Leadership is shared in the classroom; students facilitate the daily operation of the classroom.

Students share classroom responsibilities; all students become integral parts of the management of the classroom.

The desire for positive relationships governs classroom behavior and creates the context for a willingness to change behavior.

Consequences reflect individual differences.

Management is a form of guidance.

Teachers view conflict as an opportunity to connect with and teach children about relationships and standards.

Rewards are mostly intrinsic.

Discipline comes from the self.

cooperative climates. Moreover, because many of their phi-
losophies originate from a democratic view of education—
that through classroom activities, students learn to be good
citizens—relationship-based management models provide
children with opportunities to assume responsibilities for collective classroom problems and practice having a voice and
making changes in their classroom communities.

ESPOUSING A RELATIONAL VIEW OF CLASSROOM MANAGEMENT

Throughout this book, we review theory and research that
makes the case for adopting a relational view of classroom
management. That is, we believe that classroom management practices need to be developmental, acknowledging
students' emerging understanding of adult, peer, and power
relationships, and involving students in serving as leaders
and sharing the responsibility for the daily operation of the
classroom. This view acknowledges that students of all ages
will come to the classroom with varying understandings of
how to interact with adults and with their peers and may
violate teachers' norms. We then translate this research into
reflective tools that teachers can use to implement relational
management strategies in their classroom. A relational view
of classroom management argues that when students behave
in ways that create conflict for teachers or peers, they do so
in an attempt to meet their needs. Understanding students'
developmental needs; designing a management plan that
allows for students to meet their needs to feel competent,
autonomous, and connected to their teacher and peers; and
seeking to understand (mis)behavior as a function of need
fulfillment are important steps to managing a classroom that
allows for students to develop critical thinking, problem
solving, and leadership skills. Relational views of classroom
management often fall outside mainstream practices
endorsed by schools and districts. We offer this text as an
invitation to teachers who feel dissatisfied with current

practices and who are questioning why the practices they are using may or may not be working as they intend. We offer case studies and observations from our own experiences and of teachers we have observed and interviewed at different phases of their careers. The teachers in our cases are each questioning their practices. We offer reflective activities and tools for collecting classroom data that can lead to meaningful change in classroom practice.

Again, it is important to note there are several relationship-based classroom management programs that have been implemented throughout the country for young children (Bailey, 2000), elementary age students (Watson & Ecken, 2003), and adolescents (Frieberg, 1999b). We believe the efficacy of these programs lies in understanding the theoretical rationales that drive pedagogical decisions. For this reason, in lieu of describing these programs in a single chapter, we have chosen to integrate information about these programs in each chapter.

Throughout this book, educators will learn how to apply the following concepts to their classroom practices:

- Custodial and humanistic management beliefs
- Student behavioral, relational, and cognitive engagement
- Alignment of classroom management plans with instructional pedagogies
- Classroom structures that contribute to student engagement
- Beliefs that affect teacher-student relationship quality and student learning
- Immediacy behaviors that contribute to relationship quality
- The contribution of peer relationships to positive and negative behavior management
- Classroom management to accommodate developmental differences in motivation
- Strategies that help children learn to manage their own behavior
- Cultural synchronization

- The principles of self-regulatory theory and their relationships to planning, instruction, documentation, and assessment practices
- Ways to systematically and productively reflect on classroom relationships and the efficacy of their management practices

Our case studies offer snapshots of five different teachers at critical points in their careers. What they share in common is a deep commitment to building relationships with their students, but they offer different perspectives on how classroom relationships should operate. Often the teachers (including Lauren) are struggling to make sense of what is happening in their classrooms or in specific relationships with children. Each case is designed to reveal the challenges we face to build a network of classroom relationships that optimizes engagement for all students. We offer reflective questions throughout each chapter as a way to help clarify each teacher's perspective as well as your own.

CONNECTING WITH ALL STUDENTS

We recognize that a discussion of classroom management would be incomplete if we did not address the issues of disruptive student behavior. Disruptive student behaviors have been recognized as the top reason contributing to teachers' feelings of burnout. In 1995, Friedman published a report on the types of behavior problems that contribute to teacher burnout. Among the most frequently cited disruptive behaviors were talking out of turn (23%), hostility toward peers or teacher (21%), and an inattentiveness or unwillingness to learn (27%). The literature on teacher burnout is clear. Teachers need a resource for thinking about classroom management issues— one grounded in theory and empirical research and that maintains the focus on student learning. Our goal is to provide educators with ideas and methods that allow teachers to *plan for* and *respond to* classroom disruptions and relational conflict.

In 1998, Martin, Yin, and Baldwin found teachers' responses to classroom management problems fell into three categories:

1. Interactions needed to facilitate orderly and organized instruction

2. Interactions needed to facilitate the development of supportive classroom relationships

3. Interactions designed to prevent and respond to student (mis)behavior

How teachers dealt with each type of interaction largely depended on how they defined *discipline* and the self-imposed boundaries they established. To facilitate orderly and organized instruction, teachers tend to establish spatial and temporal boundaries dictating when and where different lessons will be learned. To facilitate the development of supportive classroom relationships, teachers tend to establish relational boundaries concerning with whom and how members of the class will interact. And in order to prevent and respond to student (mis)behavior, teachers tend to establish definitions of what constitutes a problem behavior. Our judgments of what constitutes a problem behavior, however, often reflect our own needs to feel competent as teachers, in control of the classroom, and connected to our students (Andrzejewski & Davis, 2008; Newberry & Davis, 2008).

REDEFINING *DISCIPLINE*

From a relational perspective, then, how do we judge problem behavior? And how do we define discipline? In a traditional model of classroom management, any behavior that defies the norms and standards established by the teacher is a problem that requires disciplinary action by the teacher. *In contrast to a traditional model where discipline is performed by the teacher, in a relational model, discipline is a collective process* (see Figure 0.1). Students are encouraged *and* provided opportunities to develop their sense of competence for solving social and academic problems and meeting their own needs. Problems are reflected in relational conflict (i.e., between the teacher and a student or between the students) but represent opportunities for learning about each other's needs. Through observing how teachers manage conflict and through opportunities for children to participate as leaders and problem solvers children learn that

a. they can be in charge of their own learning and relationships

b. they have the power to solve social and academic problems

c. although they are responsible for their own feelings, their choices impact others

d. conflict is a part of life

e. you can teach other people how to treat you

f. caring and love are more powerful than coercion and fear (Bailey, 2000, p. 13)

One of our goals when envisioning this book was to extend the work by Brophy and colleagues (1996) on problem students. We believe children who engage in disruptive behavior need compassion from their teachers—including displays of affection to show they care (Oplatka, 2007). "These children find it hard to believe their teachers really care about them, despite the evidence that they do" (Watson & Ecken, 2003, p. 3). Without compassion, problem students are likely to become alienated from their teachers (Finn, 1989) and feel less motivated in school (Cornelius-White, 2008). We believe one of the challenges teachers face is to avoid habitually judging student behavior in an unproductive way (Chang & Davis, 2009). In Chapter 4, we help teachers to identify unproductive "trigger thoughts" (Bailey, 2000, p. 31) that can lead teachers toward more *interactionist* and *interventionist* reactions. And we devote time in our final chapters to providing resources for teachers to intervene in alienated or conflicted relationships in ways that promote feelings of competence, autonomy, and connection for both teachers and students.

We also address the kinds of conflicts teachers experience with students who hail from different backgrounds than their own (Chapter 6, How Do I Connect With Diverse Students?) and the kinds of conflicts teachers experience with students who process information and learn in systematically different ways (Chapter 7, What Does It Mean to Self-Regulate My Classroom Management Tasks?) in separate chapters. We do this because issues of culture and social-historical context often lie under the surface of our consciousness and shape our interactions in ways that we may overlook. We wanted to bring to awareness the ways in which our methods of interacting and the conflicts we experience with children and youth can be shaped by larger discourses and systems in society. But strategies from across each of the chapters are designed to inform each other. We envision readers being able to bounce between chapters and assemble a set of tools that meets their individual classroom needs.

CONNECT TO YOUR PRACTICE

Reflect on Your Beliefs About Classroom Management

The Pupil Control Ideology (PCI) survey was one of the earliest approaches to conceptualizing and assessing perspectives on discipline (Hoy, 2001; Willower, Eidell, & Hoy, 1967). It is publicly available and has been used by researchers for more than 40 years to understand how teachers' management beliefs affect student achievement (http://www.waynekhoy.com/pupil_control.html).

We adapted 16 of the items from the PCI to use as a reflective tool allowing you to evaluate your own beliefs about student behavior (see Figure 0.2). Consider this a preassessment, allowing you to identify your initial orientation toward classroom discipline. Respond honestly to each item. Then use the scoring rubric at the end to calculate scores for each dimension.

What do the scores tell you about your orientation toward classroom management? Where might these beliefs have originated? How do you see these beliefs enacted in your current classroom management practices?

Figure 0.2   The Pupil Control Ideology (PCI) Survey

The single greatest factor that leads to teacher burnout is dealing with student behavior (Friedman, 1995). Look at the statements below and decide on a scale of *1= Never true* to *6 = Always true* the extent to which the statement reflects your belief about the nature of classroom management.

	Never true		Sometimes true		Always true	
1. It is more important for my students to learn to obey rules than to make their own decision...................	1	2	3	4	5	6
2. My students can be trusted to work together without supervision..	1	2	3	4	5	6
3. Being friendly with my students often leads them to become too familiar.................................	1	2	3	4	5	6
4. It is important to me to try to understand the reasons for my students' misbehavior...................	1	2	3	4	5	6
5. If my students use obscene or profane language at school, I consider it a moral offense.......................	1	2	3	4	5	6
6. I respect the ideas of my students even when I do not agree with them................................	1	2	3	4	5	6
7. Too much of our class time is already spent on guidance activities at the expense of my students' academic preparation..................................	1	2	3	4	5	6
8. I believe establishing mutual respect and understanding is more effective than establishing controlling structures in ensuring effective classroom discipline...	1	2	3	4	5	6
9. In my experience, students often misbehave in order to make their teacher look bad....................	1	2	3	4	5	6
10. In my experience, empathizing with students will enhance their trust in me..............................	1	2	3	4	5	6
11. I find it is often necessary to remind my students that their status in school affects mine....................	1	2	3	4	5	6
12. I would like to treat my students as friends so that we can be close to each other.......................	1	2	3	4	5	6
13. In my experience every class has a few students who are just young bullies and should be treated accordingly...	1	2	3	4	5	6
14. My students can distinguish between right and wrong and behave appropriately...........................	1	2	3	4	5	6
15. In my experience, student governments are good safety valves, but should not have that much influence on school policy...........................	1	2	3	4	5	6
16. I believe my students should be given the maximum opportunity to express themselves in our classroom...	1	2	3	4	5	6

Calculate your score on the odd items: Custodial beliefs

Calculate your score on the even items: Humanistic beliefs

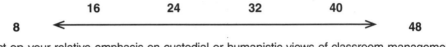

Reflect on your relative emphasis on custodial or humanistic views of classroom management. Do your intuitive beliefs about classroom management lean more toward custodial or humanistic?

How do you see these beliefs enacted in your current classroom?

KEY TERMS

Custodial management orientation: An approach to classroom management in which the teacher's role is to maintain control and order in the classroom.

Discipline: The reactions of a teacher to any student behavior that does not align with the expectations and norms the teacher has established for the classroom.

Humanistic management orientation: An approach to classroom management in which the teacher's role is to create a classroom environment in which students can learn to self-regulate and control their own behavior and relationships.

Relationship-based management approaches: Classroom management practice in which the teacher encourages each student to take shared ownership of the classroom environment and their behavior and in which behavioral expectations are adjusted to meet the needs of each student.

Traditional management approaches: Classroom management practice in which the teacher is the sole creator and enforcer of rules, rewards, and consequences.

RESOURCES FOR TEACHERS

Bailey, B. A. (2000). *Conscious discipline: 7 basic skills for brain smart classroom management.* Oviedo, FL: Loving Guidance. [See also http://www.consciousdiscipline.com/]

Brophy, J. (1999). Perspectives of classroom management: Yesterday, today, tomorrow. In H. J. Frieberg (Ed.), *Beyond behaviorism: Changing the classroom management paradigm* (pp. 43–56). Boston, MA: Allyn & Bacon.

Fisher, B. (1998). *Joyful learning in kindergarten.* Westport, CT: Greenwood/Heinemann.

Frieberg, H. J. (1999a). Beyond behaviorism. In H. J. Frieberg (Ed.), *Beyond behaviorism: Changing the classroom management paradigm* (pp. 3–20). Boston, MA: Allyn & Bacon.

Frieberg, H. J. (1999b). Consistency management & cooperative discipline: From tourists to citizens in the classroom. In H. J. Frieberg (Ed.), *Beyond* behaviorism: Changing the classroom management paradigm (pp. 75–97). Boston, MA: Allyn & Bacon. [See also http://cmcd.coe.uh.edu/]

Kratochwill, T. (n.d.). Classroom management [Teacher module]. Retrieved from http://www.apa.org/education/k12/classroom-mgmt.aspx

Scherer, M. (Ed.). (2009). Engaging the whole child: Reflections on best practices in learning, teaching, and leadership. Alexandria, VA: Association for Supervision and Curriculum Development.

Tharpe, R. G., Estrada, P., Dalton, S. S., & Yamauchi, L. A. (2000). Teaching transformed; achieving excellence, fairness, inclusion and harmony. Boulder, CO: Westview Press.

Watson, M., & Ecken, L. (2003). Learning to trust: Transforming difficult elementary classrooms through developmental discipline. Hoboken, NJ: Jossey-Bass.

Weissberg, R. P., Kumpfer, K., & Seligman, M. E. P. (Eds.). (2003). Prevention that works for children and youth: An introduction. American Psychologist, 58, 425–432. [Key work for social and emotional learning]

Wolfgang, C. (1999). Solving discipline problems: Methods and models for today's teachers. Boston, MA: Allyn & Bacon.

PART I

Management as a Function of Student Engagement

1

What Does It Mean for Students to Be Engaged?

T eachers are constantly working to connect their students to school and to learning because they know that engagement is crucial to school success. It may help teachers to know that school engagement occurs on multiple levels. Addressing each level of engagement can increase the chances that a teacher can sustain his or her students' engagement. The definition of school engagement is complex, and there has been some disagreement with regard to the number of theoretical dimensions. Some scholars argue for two dimensions (i.e., behavioral and emotional; see Finn & Voelkl, 1993; Skinner & Belmont, 1993), and other scholars argue for three dimensions (i.e., behavioral, emotional, and cognitive; see Fredricks, Blumenfeld, & Paris, 2004). We argue that teachers need to think about engagement as encompassing three interconnected dimensions: *behavioral engagement*, *cognitive engagement*, and *relational engagement* (see Figure 1.1). We

Figure 1.1 Three Interconnected Dimensions: Behavioral Engagement, Cognitive Engagement, and Relational Engagement

Relational Engagement

The quality of students' interactions in the classroom and school community

How do students' ways of relating to their teachers and peers affect their motivation, performance, and understanding of academic content?

Cognitive Engagement

The quality of students' psychological engagement in academic tasks, including their interest, ownership, and strategies for learning

How do students' emotional and cognitive investment in the learning process affect their performance and understanding of academic content?

Behavioral Engagement

The quality of students' participation in the classroom and school community

How do students' patterns of behavior and participation in the classroom affect their motivation, performance, and understanding of academic content?

believe **relational engagement** is most relevant to classroom management that promotes optimal engagement in school.

THREE TYPES OF ENGAGEMENT

Consider the student who always works hard but still seems to struggle with learning. This student may be behaviorally engaged but not cognitively engaged. Scholars tend to agree that **behavioral engagement** encompasses students' effort, persistence, participation, and compliance with school structures. In general, school-level changes are typically focused on modifying students' behavioral engagement. Achievement in school is often included in the research as an outcome of students' behavioral engagement as measured by teacher or self-reports of students' effort (e.g., including daily/weekly grades for classroom/lab participation and homework completion and task persistence; Davis, Shalter-Bruening, & Andrzejewski, 2008).

Cognitive engagement is a matter of students' will—that is, how students feel about themselves and their work, their skills, and the strategies they employ to master their work (Metallidou & Viachou, 2007). Teachers may be familiar with the student who always works hard but still seems unable to learn effectively. This student also may be behaviorally engaged but not cognitively engaged. In other words, just because students appear to be working on the task at hand does not mean they are learning. It is important to note that effort is involved in both behavioral and cognitive definitions of engagement: "In this sense, cognitive engagement refers to the quality of students' engagement whereas sheer effort refers to the quantity of their engagement in the class" (Pintrich, 2003, p. 105). The inclusion of cognitive engagement makes an important distinction between students' efforts to simply do the work and effort that is focused on understanding and mastery (Fredricks et al., 2004; Greene, Miller, Crowson, Duke, & Akey, 2004). Students who are cognitively *and* behaviorally engaged will attend to the task at hand and simultaneously manage their learning (e.g., thinking about similar tasks they have done, realizing when they need to ask for help, using problem-solving strategies).

> Reflect on the common activities you assign students in your class. What are the characteristics of activities that promote both behavioral *and* cognitive engagement?

While the concepts of cognitive and behavioral engagement are well understood in the context of previous research (Fredericks et al., 2004), there is little consistency in the way in which **emotional engagement** has been defined by educational researchers. For example, in their study of the ways in which classroom structures affected students' emotional engagement, Skinner and Belmont (1993) defined emotional engagement as students' feelings of interest, happiness, anxiety, and anger during achievement-related activities. In contrast, Sciarra and Seirup (2008) defined emotional engagement as the extent to which students feel a sense of **belonging** "and the degree to which they care about their school" (p. 218). Emotional engagement from their perspective has more to do with the pleasant and unpleasant emotions students connect to their relationships with teachers, peers, and school rather than the feelings they have during learning activities. In a recent study by Davis, Chang, Andrzejewski, and Poirier (2010), the researchers argued that previous definitions of emotional engagement, like that of Sciarra and Seirup, may actually be referring to **relational engagement**. Specifically, Davis et al. used students' reports of perceived teacher support, perceived press for understanding (i.e., students' perception that the teacher wants them to learn and understand), and their sense of school belonging as proxies for understanding the extent to which students were relationally engaged in school.

What would a student who is relationally engaged in the classroom look like? Within the research literature on motivation, several theoretical and empirical models include aspects of relational engagement, such as Reeve's research of teacher **autonomy support** and motivation (Jang, Reeve, & Deci, 2010; Reeve, 2006, 2009; Reeve & Jang, 2006; Reeve, Jang, Carrell, Jeon, & Barch, 2004), Middleton's study of academic goals and press for understanding (Middleton & Midgley, 2002), and Goodenow's (1992, 1993a, 1993b) work on school belonging and motivation in urban populations. However, some of the most comprehensive theories that capture the multiple facets of relational engagement are motivational systems theory and self-determination theory.

> Think about your classroom. What could relational engagement look like in your classroom?
>
> To what extent do the students in Alice's and Kim's classes appear to be behaviorally, cognitively, and relationally engaged?

MOTIVATIONAL SYSTEMS THEORY

Originated by Ford (1992), motivational systems theory (or MST) proposes that effective functioning or **competence** can best be defined as the attainment of personally and/or socially valued goals (1992, 1996). Goals are attained if the following prerequisites are met:

1. The person has the motivation needed to initiate and maintain activity directed toward a goal.

2. The person has the skill needed to construct and execute a pattern of activity that is appropriate and effective with respect to those outcomes.

3. The person's biological structure and functioning is able to support both the motivational and skill components.

4. There is a responsive environment facilitating progress toward a goal.

Within the first prerequisite, it is assumed that goals, emotions, and personal agency beliefs (i.e., beliefs that one has control over learning the activity) work together to guide decision making, including to support caring behavior. Ford argues that caring behavior, what we might label as an important aspect of relational engagement, provides a strong motivational foundation for cognitive and behavioral engagement in school contexts. In other words, students who care for each other and perceive that they are in a caring environment are motivated to engage cognitively and behaviorally. Theoretically, the personal goals most relevant to caring behavior are four integrative social relationship goals: *belongingness, social responsibility, equity,* and *resource provision* (Ford & Nichols, 1987, 1991). Students who are able to work successfully toward these goals typically say that caring for and about others is always, or almost always, important. It is important for educators to be aware of each of these social relationship goals.

Belongingness goals are defined as building or maintaining attachments, friendships, or a sense of community. Maintaining or enhancing a sense of belongingness with teachers or successful peers can facilitate school achievement (Connell & Wellborn, 1991) and positive adjustment in school (Van Ryzin, Gravely, & Roset, 2009). **Social responsibility goals** are defined as keeping interpersonal commitments, meeting social role obligations, and conforming to social and moral rules. Like belongingness, social responsibility goals also appear to provide the motivational foundation needed to facilitate positive school adjustment (i.e., liking school, having friends in school) and academic achievement (Wentzel, 1991a, 1991b, 1993, 1994, 1998). One of the ways teachers can increase students' sense of belongingness and social responsibility is to develop positive peer relationships by using cooperative learning structures in the classroom (Hijzen, Boekaerts, & Vedder, 2007). This instructional method will be explored further in Chapter 5. Another means of increasing students' sense of belonging is to develop positive relationships with their teacher (Davis, 2003, 2006). These student-teacher relational processes will be explored further in Chapter 4.

Equity goals are defined as promoting fairness, justice, reciprocity, or equality. According to Dover's (2009) review, several different studies found that teachers who incorporated the following principles of social justice instruction in their classrooms had high levels of academic engagement, created learning communities that encouraged social cooperation among students, and increased overall performance:

1. Assume all students are participants in knowledge constructions, have high expectations for students and themselves, and foster learning communities.

2. Acknowledge, value, and build upon students' existing knowledge, interests, cultural, and linguistic resources.

3. Teach specific academic skills and bridge gaps in students' learning.

Resource provision is defined as giving approval, support, assistance, advice, or validation to others. Resource provision goals can be embedded in social relationships that are reciprocal (i.e., peer-to-peer relationships) or in asymmetrical social roles where one person is responsible for providing resources to another (i.e., teacher-student relationships). Many of the intervention strategies to reduce general aggression and bullying behavior in schools focus on helping students develop social competence and empathy skills toward other students, which are forms of resource provision. Some of these strategies will be reviewed in Chapter 5.

Think about your own classroom.

To what extent do students have an opportunity to belong?

To what extent do students have an opportunity to behave in socially responsible ways?

To what extent do students have an opportunity to promote fairness and experience reciprocity?

To what extent do students have an opportunity to serve as resources for you and their peers?

SELF-DETERMINATION THEORY

Self-determination theory emphasizes the significance of three basic psychological needs in people's self-motivation and healthy psychological growth—the needs for competence, **relatedness**, and **autonomy**. According to self-determination theory, social-contextual conditions that provide people with the opportunity to satisfy their basic needs lead to enhanced motivation, optimal functioning, and psychological well-being (Deci & Ryan, 2000; Ryan & Deci, 2000). Therefore, when teachers and classrooms support the satisfaction of student needs, students will feel *self-determined*. Need for *relatedness*, or a basic need to be connected or related to others, is most relevant to our understanding of relational engagement. There is not as much research that focuses on relatedness as the other two basic needs for autonomy and competence in the classroom, but the research that exists focuses on teachers' emotional support for students (Connell & Wellborn, 1991; Ryan, Stiller, & Lynch, 1994; Skinner & Belmont, 1993; Wentzel, 1997, 1998) rather than on students' caring for each other. For example, in a recent study by Nie and Lau (2009), teacher caring, or involvement, predicted students' emotional and behavioral engagement and satisfaction with school. Nie and Lau also found that the teacher's ability to manage his or her classroom was an important predictor of emotional engagement. In a similar study, Furrer and Skinner (2003) also demonstrated the relationship between students' feelings of relatedness and behavioral engagement, but they took into account that students have relatedness needs from specific social partners—namely parents, teachers, and peers. Furrer and Skinner suggested that more research is needed to discover how children achieve a sense of relatedness with peers and how schools can facilitate this process.

> Consider the students in your classroom.
> What are (might be) their relational needs?
> What are your relational needs as their teacher?

WHY IS RELATIONAL ENGAGEMENT IMPORTANT?

We believe that the components of integrative social relationship goals described above are very much in line with our definition of relational engagement. In particular, students who have positive social relationship goals tend to care about others in ways that predict their ability to be successful in social situations, such as classrooms. In an empirical study of caring competence, or ability to care, Ford and his colleagues (Ford, Love, Chase, Pollina, & Ito, as cited in Ford, 1996) found that students' caring competence was positively correlated with all four integrative social relationship goals: belongingness, equity, social responsibility, and resource provision. Most of the students in the high-caring group had high scores on measures of belongingness, resource provision, and empathic concern. In other words, the profile of a caring student has strong resource provision goals, compelling feelings of empathic concern and pride or pleasure in helping others, and positive capability beliefs for caring action. Compared to the low-caring students, high-caring students were more likely to be interested in a diversity of personal goals that were both social and nonsocial, including intellectual goals and creativity goals. Therefore, it seems that teachers should be able to increase students' ability to care by acting on goals related to belongingness, social responsibility, equity, and resource provision. Similarly, teachers can help students meet their relatedness needs in the classroom in order for them to be optimally engaged in the learning process (Furrer & Skinner, 2003).

WHAT TEACHERS CAN DO TO SUPPORT CARING AND STUDENTS' RELATEDNESS NEEDS

It would be easy to say that teachers need to develop a sense of caring and relatedness in their classrooms by emphasizing a sense of community, but how does one begin to do that? With a unique perspective on developing learning community, Heck

(2004) uses Paula Underwood's Native American Learning Stories (2002, as cited in Heck):

> I use these stories to enrich my classroom content with narrative and cultural diversity, nurture my dispositions toward others who seem difficult or puzzling, and expand my abilities to develop meaningful learning environments and experiences. The stories readily enhance, rather than detract from, curricular goals and state standards, while engaging students in active and critical thinking about relationships with others. (p. 36)

Although these stories are not specifically designed to help teachers with classroom management, they offer a holistic way of learning by participating in relational engagement activities. Specifically, Heck suggests that Underwood's stories can be used to teach caring about another's voice (see also Noddings, 1995). Each story addresses the following pedagogical dilemmas outlined by Adams (1997, as cited in Heck, p. 41):

1. The challenge of balancing the emotional and cognitive demands of the learning process

2. The challenge of acknowledging and supporting the subjective contexts (how students make meaning out of their own individual experiences) while illuminating the systemic contexts (the demands of moving between social groups) that affect learning

3. The challenge of attending to students' social relationships in the classroom

4. The challenge of balancing personal reflection with regular observations of their experiences as tools for fostering student-centered learning

5. The challenge of valuing awareness, personal growth, and change as meaningful outcomes of the learning process

If we revisit the case of how Alice and Kim manage their classrooms, described in the introduction, one might come to the conclusion that Alice is trying to address these dilemmas by using a relational engagement approach to classroom management. Alice clearly appears more interested in helping her students "care" for one another by teaching them skills associated with caring competence (Ford & Nichols, 1991), which will hopefully facilitate students' positive social relationship goals in her classroom and in the long run.

KEY TERMS

Autonomy: A student's feelings of independence or freedom to make his or her own decisions; one of the three components of self-determination theory.

Autonomy supportive: A classroom environment that supports the development of student autonomy by giving students more opportunities to make their own decisions and choices.

Behavioral engagement: A student's effort, persistence, participation, and compliance with school/classroom rules and structures.

Belongingness goals: The desire to build and maintain friendships or a sense of community with others.

Cognitive engagement: A student's completion of academic tasks and monitoring of his or her own learning habits.

Competence: A student's confidence in his or her abilities; one of the three components of self-determination theory.

Emotional engagement: A student's positive emotions related to school activities.

Equity goals: The desire to promote values such as fairness, justice, or equality in society.

CONNECT TO YOUR PRACTICE

Reflect on High- and Low-Caring Students' Attempts to Meet Relatedness Needs

Students' pursuits of social goals in classrooms can vary widely across classrooms and can look different depending on whether they are a high- or low-caring student. Spend a week observing the social goal pursuit of two students in your class. Identify a high-caring and low-caring student to observe. Make note of the different ways the students pursue their needs to acquire the resources they need to learn, to be treated equitably, to behave responsibly, and to feel like they belong in the classroom.

Social Goal Pursuit	High-Caring Student	Low-Caring Student
Resource provision		
Equity		
Social responsibility		
Belongingness		

Relatedness/belonging: A student's feelings of being connected or related to others; one of the three components of self-determination theory.

Relational engagement: A student's feelings of being supported, pushed to learn, and accepted at school.

Resource provision: The giving of approval, support, assistance, advice, or validation to others, whether in a peer-to-peer relationship or a teacher-student relationship.

Self-determination theory: A theory that holds that students' ability to be self-motivated depends on whether or not their needs for competence, relatedness, and autonomy are satisfied.

Social responsibility goals: The desire to meet social norms, such as having friends.

RESOURCES FOR TEACHERS

Educators for Social Responsibility: http://www.esrnational.org/otc/
Self-Determination Theory: http://www.psych.rochester.edu/SDT/
Wentzel, K. R. (2003). Motivating students to behave in socially competent ways. *Theory Into Practice, 42,* 319–326.

2

How Do I Organize My Classroom for Engagement?

A s educators, we all know the foundation of effective instruction and classroom management is planning. When we've planned well, our lessons run smoothly. We feel able to anticipate problems, perhaps even viewing some of the problems our students encounter as natural and functional. And we conclude lessons feeling like we accomplished the tasks we set forth. The biggest challenge with planning, however, is taking a holistic view of our instructional design to incorporate both the immediate objectives posed by a daily lesson and the more global developmental objectives we espouse as teachers.

The foundation of all classroom management programs, both traditional and relational, is anticipation and prevention. Thus, teachers are encouraged to structure the environment around the goals of optimal student engagement first and nurture the child second. In this chapter, we'll overview three different perspectives on instructional design. Next, we'll deconstruct the planning process into three different components: planning to promote behavioral and relational engagement, planning to promote cognitive engagement, and planning to promote the development of students' autonomy and responsibility in the classroom.

INSTRUCTIONAL DESIGN: CONSISTENCY MANAGEMENT

Frieberg (1999a, 1999b) developed the term **consistency management** to refer to all of the instructional planning that we engage in to ensure our students are optimally engaged. Consistency management encompasses everything from the macro decisions we make such as mission statements we write about the kind of classroom we want to the micro decisions we make concerning the routines and behavioral expectations we convey for individual activities. The emphasis is on creating structures in the classroom that enable students to anticipate what will happen next. Consistency management can include prevention measures such as articulating clear expectations about how to behave during an activity. However, it also encompasses all of the ways in which we systematically integrate opportunities for our students to develop a sense of responsibility for their own learning and leadership skills in the classroom.

Often, the challenge with consistency management is aligning our instructional pedagogy with our classroom management. As most states transition toward 21st century learning standards that incorporate innovative methods and new technologies, students need to develop the skills to work collaboratively, regulate their own behavior, and solve challenging, ambiguous problems. In 1992, Jere Brophy and Mary McCaslin published a seminal piece in which they argued that traditional classroom management practices were undermining our abilities to promote the highest levels of cognitive engagement in our students. They argued that students were learning compliant cognition practices; that is, students were learning that in order to be successful in school, they needed to reiterate what their teachers and textbooks were saying. In becoming behaviorally compliant, students were losing their own voices in the classroom, silencing their true thoughts and feelings and responding with politeness and acquiescence. Moreover, in teaching students to be cognitively compliant, teachers may undermine their ability to teach students how to cope with stress and frustration and the ability to frame and solve problems. Traditional forms of classroom management, based on behavioral control, afford students the fewest opportunities to not only develop their own abilities to self-regulate their learning but also to develop their abilities to think and problem solve for themselves. Essentially, because teachers generate the rules, establish the **class norms**, and are the sole evaluators and providers of feedback and praise, students learn implicitly that they are not, and cannot, be in control of their own behavior and must rely on someone else to judge the quality of their thinking work in school. For example, in her case study of the transition to high school, Cyrene Wells (1996) found, "Students' frustrations were largely hidden under a cover of politeness and acquiescence. For instance, even though the students . . . alternately despised, feared, and tolerated [one of their teachers] and didn't believe they were learning that much—they didn't directly challenge him. They understood that it would make no difference, except perhaps to make things worse" (p. 133).

> Reflect on your instructional and classroom management pedagogies. Are they sending students a consistent message about the importance of critical thinking and problem solving?

In traditional classroom management models, behavioral and verbal transgressions are treated with punishment or dismissal to time out or the principal's office. Imagine the tension students must feel when their teachers tell them during an activity, "I want to know what you think." But every time they inappropriately express an unpleasant emotion (e.g., anger, frustration, disappointment, boredom) we tell them they are not allowed to feel that way. In order to protect themselves, students learn to resolve this conflict by concealing their thoughts and emotions from their teachers.

Relational forms of classroom management can adopt two different approaches to managing student behavior: co-regulated and self-regulated. In co-regulated classrooms, students and teachers work together to create a set of negotiated norms (e.g., classroom rules) and to establish learning goals for the year. In doing so, teachers create opportunities for students to develop a set of internal behavioral standards and to identify learning goals that reflect their interests. Teachers assist students in reflecting on the work they produce and involve them in providing feedback. In doing so, teachers create opportunities for students to develop a set of internal standards regarding the quality of work to be produced and enable them to develop an internal voice that can describe how they think and feel about the work. Consistency management in this type of classroom involves establishing expectations for working together to solve problems. Interpersonal conflict is not viewed as a problem, but as a learning opportunity.

In self-regulated classrooms, teachers serve as conduits for assisting students in understanding how they learn, and they enable students in monitoring their own learning and development. As with co-regulated classrooms, students are involved in establishing goals for their learning. In self-regulated classrooms, the emphasis is placed on the following:

1. Helping students identify goals for instruction

2. Helping students monitor the efficacy of the strategies they use for learning

3. Helping students learn to "talk themselves through" (McCaslin et al., 2006, p. 226) problems

4. Helping students frame failures in terms of the planning and/or strategies they employed

In both co-regulated and self-regulated classrooms, there is a meaningful place for failed attempts and conflict. Lyn Corno and colleagues (Corno & Snow, 1986; Rohrkemper & Corno, 1988) argue that adaptive learners know how to manage the emotional stress of not immediately understanding a problem, failing the first time, and changing the plan of action. Teachers attempting to design for a self-regulated classroom try to anticipate *where* students will experience meaningful or "functional failures" and build that into their activities. Consistency management in this type of classroom involves establishing expectations for students that enable them to understand the meaning and purpose of conflict, constructive failure, and repeating attempts at problem solving.

The challenge with co-regulated and self-regulated classrooms, however, is that we have to invest time and energy at the beginning of the year teaching students how to behave in more complex learning environments. This involves explaining the norms for appropriate behavior (i.e., during group time, during transitions between activities, when there is a problem with technology) so that our students develop a thorough understanding of the purpose of classroom norms.

In 1997, Mary Manke published a year-long case study of power dynamics in an elementary classroom. She argued that no matter what kind of instructional design we plan, there will always be seams in our instructional design. These **seams in instruction** represent the times and spaces in our classrooms when students attempt to exert their autonomy and control the classroom dynamic. Manke observed how elementary students, when denied opportunities for autonomy, exerted their power by interrupting the teacher, disrupting their peers, and subverting activities. Ultimately, there are tradeoffs with each approach to classroom management. With a traditional approach, teachers can establish an instructional design with the fewest seams: They can plan for transitions between activities and clearly explain behavioral expectations. However, even with the most tightly sewn seams, students can pick away and unravel activities in their attempts to meet their needs for autonomy. In contrast, self-regulated classrooms may have the most seams in instruction; teachers are more likely to spend their management time instructing students in how to approach tasks, cope with task-related emotions, and interact with other students and with the teacher. However, because these seams are more loosely sewn and may have been negotiated with students, behavioral and verbal transgressions are less likely to feel like acts of defiance.

> Consider Alice's and Kim's classrooms.
> What forms of regulation do you see?
> Are their classrooms examples of co-regulation or self-regulation?

ORGANIZING FOR STUDENT AUTONOMY

How much student autonomy do you build into your management plan? This is a challenging question to answer because it depends on your knowledge of your students. Younger children, who have had the least experience with behavioral norms and academic contexts, are more likely to need a co-regulated management structure where teachers work with students to negotiate classroom norms and behavioral expectations for tasks. In Figure 2.1, we provide an example of a set of classroom rules negotiated on the first day of preschool. The children were asked to think about the kinds of things everyone in the class needed to do in order for the classroom to be a safe, healthy, learning space. It is important to remember in co-regulated classrooms that the class may need to revisit, renegotiate, and redefine each rule as the year progresses. For example, children may come to the classroom with different understandings of what it means to share.

Inevitably, preschool children will struggle with sharing because this is a concept they are learning. In a co-regulated classroom, after the teacher has observed several occasions where students have had trouble sharing, he or she draws his or her class's attention back to the list of rules and asks them, "I notice that we are having some trouble sharing, and I wonder if we all understand sharing the same way. What does it mean to you to share?"

With adolescents, negotiating principles at the start of the year can take the form of a classroom constitution (Frieberg,

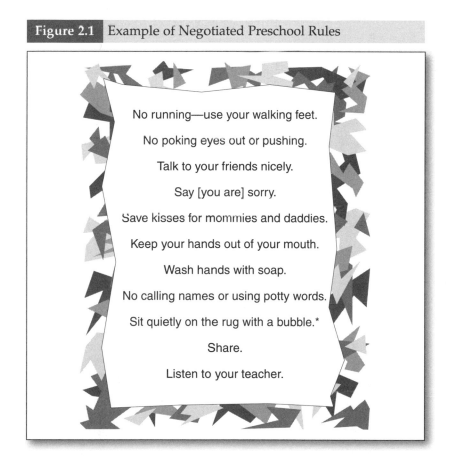

| Figure 2.1 | Example of Negotiated Preschool Rules |

No running—use your walking feet.

No poking eyes out or pushing.

Talk to your friends nicely.

Say [you are] sorry.

Save kisses for mommies and daddies.

Keep your hands out of your mouth.

Wash hands with soap.

No calling names or using potty words.

Sit quietly on the rug with a bubble.*

Share.

Listen to your teacher.

* "With a bubble" refers to holding a pocket of air in your mouth so your cheeks puff out. This was the class's creative way of identifying a behavior that would signal to the teacher they were listening.

1999b), a statement about what the instructional goals will be and to which rights students and teachers are entitled. Students are often very insightful about what they perceive they need to be successful learners. Conversations about support and respect can reveal the ways in which students are making sense of these constructs and provide opportunities for us to share what we need in order to be effective teachers.

In the following sections, we outline ways in which teachers in co-regulated and self-regulated classrooms can implement classroom structures that not only maintain a focus on behavioral, relational, and cognitive engagement but also achieve students' positive behavioral engagement without making them cognitively compliant.

PLANNING TO PROMOTE BEHAVIORAL AND RELATIONAL ENGAGEMENT: ROUTINES AND RITUALS

In 2008, the U.S. Department of Education released a report summarizing the literature on traditional effective classroom management in elementary classrooms. The report found teachers experienced the least disruptions when they had established clear expectations and routines for the following events (p. 24):

1. When students are arriving and leaving the classroom

2. When distributing materials and turning in assignments

3. When students requested help from the teacher

4. When transitioning to new activities or settings

5. During interruptions in classroom routines, such as fire drills or substitute teachers

6. When students were working independently and in groups

7. When students were returning from recess or another class (art, music, or physical education)

For middle graders and secondary students in our current culture of accountability, we could also probably add the following:

8. When students present or speak publicly

9. When students are assessed individually and in groups

10. When previewing and/or reviewing homework

This list provides a guide for the common types of seams that can occur in classrooms as Manke (1997) described and allows us to systematically anticipate the kinds of problems we might observe students having and establish **routines and rituals** with our classes that maintain a focus on learning. Routines and rituals help students to feel safe and connected in their classroom. When teachers establish routines and rituals around these seams, students not only know what to expect, they also develop a set of strategies they can enact independently. Students learn that they share in the responsibility for keeping the focus on learning. Rituals reaffirm students' belonging in the classroom and their sense of connection with their teachers and peers. Routines and rituals also allow students to process more complex information at a higher level because they do not have to spend mental energy worrying about "What's coming next?"

ESTABLISHING ROUTINES FOR ENGAGEMENT

Routines are the behavioral scripts we develop that enable students to maintain a focus on doing things that promote learning. Routines provide predictability so that children and adolescents feel safe. Each time we transition between classrooms or activities, we introduce ambiguity that can leave some students feeling vulnerable. Routines remind them that they can feel in control of what is happening; they have a place in the classroom. Routines can also focus students on global learning objectives. One of our favorite routines, developed by Becky Bailey (2000), is to establish a set of **class commitments** that students can (re)commit to each day when they enter the classroom. Commitments can be behavioral: "Today I commit to showing respect to the other students in the class." Or they can orient students toward learning outcomes: "Today, I commit to learning how to be a scientist." These commitments remind students of the purposes students and teachers share and the roles everyone plays in meeting learning goals. They can also serve as a communication tool, cuing us to the goals students feel they are struggling to accomplish. Cuing students to focus on broad objectives can be as simple as having students write their commitments in their journal each morning or placing a card with the objective next to their name in a pocket chart.

> What are the overarching
> behavioral objectives for your class?
>
> How could you get your students to commit to
> focusing on the big behavioral and/or instructional
> objectives for your class?

In Figure 2.2, we outline different classroom events that may require a routine. When establishing a routine in your classroom, it is important to have a vision of the kinds of behaviors you would like to observe in your students. It is important to remember that some students may come to our classrooms with little understanding of how to bring about the desired behaviors. When establishing a new routine, there are many considerations:

1. What behavioral skills are needed for students to participate in this routine? How can I break these behaviors down into concrete, teachable steps in the event a student struggles to perform these behaviors?

2. How can I model these skills? How can I provide a variety of examples for students to observe? Can they observe other students in the class demonstrating the

behavior? Can we read books with messages about the target behavior?

3. How can I offer opportunities for students to engage in guided and later independent practice? Do we need to engage in role-play when introducing this routine?

4. How can I build in functional failures, or learning opportunities (Rohrkemper & Corno, 1988)? How can I share my thinking about this routine including how and why I sometimes fail? How can I involve students in sharing their thinking including how and why they sometimes fail?

5. How will we deal with conflict during this routine? How will I help the students in my class construct meaning around why we need this routine to have a safe, healthy learning space in our classroom?

6. How will I prompt and cue my student to engage in this routine independently? Would it help to post something around the room (or on the smart board)? Are there key words I can use?

7. How will I give specific feedback to individual students about their ability to perform each routine?

When we begin to think about integrating technology into our classrooms and creating differentiated learning opportunities for students, our classroom learning environments can quickly become complex leaving us feeling overwhelmed by the variety of seams (Manke, 1997). Frieberg (1999b), however, argues the classroom represents the frontline where students learn how to be good citizens and that teachers actually do their students a disservice when they act as the sole managers. Instead, he argues teachers need to involve students as partners and stakeholders in the classroom. "Teachers must do more than tell students to be responsible, they need to show the trust necessary for students to take responsibility in the classroom" (p. 80). We can do this by involving our students in identifying the tasks that require organization and oversight and creating job responsibilities for them. "Classroom organization is a mutual responsibility that adds valuable

Figure 2.2 Classroom Events Requiring Routines

Behavioral Engagement	Relational Engagement	Cognitive Engagement
To what extent does the **layout** of my room allow for students to be behaviorally engaged?	To what extent does the **layout** of my room allow for students to be relationally engaged?	To what extent does the **layout** of my room allow for students to be cognitively engaged?
• Can they easily access materials they need to learn? • Have I maximized our ability to move about the room?	• Does the layout of the room communicate that we are all learning together? • Can my students reach me if they need help?	• What structures do I have that involve students in setting and (re)committing to goals, monitoring our performance, and reflecting on our strategies?
To what extent are my students meaningfully, behaviorally engaged at the **start of class?**	To what extent are my students meaningfully, relationally engaged at the **start of class?**	To what extent are my students meaningfully, cognitively engaged at the **start of class?**
• To what extent do our start-up routines focus on being present for learning? • To what extent do our start-up activities help students to (re)commit to our classroom goals?	• To what extent do our start-up routines focus on making connections with me and the other students? • To what extent to our start-up routines emphasize responsibility to the class community	• To what extent do our start-up routines create curiosity? • To what extent do our start-up routines help students develop the self-regulatory skills they need to be fully engaged in school?

Behavioral Engagement	Relational Engagement	Cognitive Engagement
How well does this **activity** provide for *each* student to be behaviorally engaged? • To what extent does this activity require students to be present and engaged in a meaningful way?	How well does this **activity** provide for *each* student to be behaviorally engaged? • To what extent does this activity require students to interact meaningfully with me and with their peers? To learn from each other?	How well does this **activity** provide for *each* student to be cognitively engaged? • To what extent have I anticipated variations in students' motivation for this activity? • To what extent have I developed routines to encourage students to generate their own motivation for activities?
To what extent are my students meaningfully, behaviorally engaged during **transitions**? • When moving into centers/cooperative groups? When interacting with technology? • To what extent do our transition routines focus on being present for learning? Help students to (re)commit to our classroom goals?	To what extent are my students meaningfully, relationally engaged during **transitions**? • To what extent do our transition routines focus on making connections with me and the other students? • To what extent to our transition routines emphasize responsibility to the class community?	To what extent are my students meaningfully, cognitively engaged during **transitions**? • To what extent do our transition routines help students develop the self-regulatory skills they need to be fully engaged in school?
How do I maintain students' behavioral engagement **when they are away** from the classroom?	How do I maintain students' relational engagement **when they are away** from the classroom?	How do I maintain students' cognitive engagement **when they are away** from the classroom?

teaching and learning time and builds student ownership and self-discipline" (p. 84). Classroom management positions will vary not only with the grade level but also the content area; they can range from passing out materials to assisting a substitute teacher. There are different ways of involving students in the management of the class. One common way is to develop a system in which each student has an opportunity to serve in *each* role. One approach is to generate a job board or job wheel students can use to rotate through positions periodically. In middle level or secondary classrooms, many of the daily routines can be student-led. In this shared responsibility model, each student has an opportunity to share in the responsibility for each type of classroom task.

In contrast, Frieberg (1999b) argues for a **distributed leadership** approach in which teachers find the best approach to managing the classroom by tapping into students' expertise, ideas, and interests. In consistency management the teacher works together with students to generate a list of responsibilities and helps them organize jobs, one per student in the class, and then students apply to serve in the preferred roles. The teacher interviews students about their interests and expertise and then assigns jobs. The jobs rotate as students' interests and expertise change.

Throughout the country, many states are implementing 1-to-1 laptop initiatives. A major concern of new teachers is how their classroom management will change when their students each have their own personal learning device. Figure 2.3 is an example of the leadership roles we use in our classrooms. Notice that five of the duties involve sharing responsibility for implementing the technology. These tasks create opportunities for students to learn about the technology (i.e., how to set up and break down presentation and recording equipment, how to post to webspace, and how to field questions about technology) and opportunities for them to demonstrate their technology knowledge and skills. When we relinquish these tasks to our students, we create time and space for instructional activities that require the teacher's fullest attention.

Figure 2.3	Examples of Distributed Leadership in a Secondary/College Classroom

1. **Room setup:** Arrange desks in discussion circle or small groups. Please arrive 2–3 minutes prior to the beginning of class to set up the room.

2. **Breakdown:** Arrange desks back into rows, erase whiteboard. Please plan on staying 2–3 minutes after class ends.

3. **Memory keeper:** Responsible for setting up flip cam at the start of class and breaking it down at the end of class. Portions of class will be uploaded to our Learning Management System (LMS) site.

4–5. **Timekeeper** (2 jobs; first and second half of class): Review agenda and monitor time for the class and instructors. Timekeepers need to be assertive: "Excuse me . . . "

6–10. **Group discussion moderator** (4–5 jobs per class): Responsible for leading the group's discussion of the articles/data.

11–15. **Group scribe** (4–5 jobs per class): Responsible for recording the synthesis of the group's discussion, presenting it to class, and posting the synthesis to the LMS site. At the beginning of the class, the group scribe should retrieve a VGA cable for projection.

16. **Technology point person:** Serve as primary contact for students when they have a question about the technology; this person will monitor the technology questions posted to the LMS site.

17. **Child development point person:** Serve as primary contact for students when they have a question about the course such as readings, postings, reflections etc.; monitor the course questions posted to the LMS site

18. **Job scribe:** Record the jobs for the following week and notify students in the class of their responsibilities. Teach the future job scribe how to record jobs.

19. **Greeter:** Responsible for connecting with each student during class to find out how he or she is doing that day. Greeters attempt to connect with students prior to the start of class and during the break. Please arrive 5–10 minutes early.

20. **Commitments scribe:** Record the commitments students worked on for that week; check in on students who reported feeling stressed. Notify instructors of absent students. Teach the future commitment scribe how to record commitments.

(Continued)

Figure 2.3 (Continued)

> 21. **Well-wisher:** Contact students who were absent (type of attendance position) and update them on what was covered in class and readings for the following week.
>
> 22. **De-stressor:** Responsible for designing a 2–3 minute activity to de-stress and refocus the class (breathing, stretching, visualization, etc.).
>
> 23. **Clarifier:** When we transition, this student is responsible for asking questions on behalf of the class and clarifying for the class his or her understanding of what will happen during transitions and when previewing homework. At the end of class, the clarifier will send an e-mail out to the class about how to be prepared for the next class.

> Consider your own classroom:
>
> What routines do you already have in place?
>
> What additional routines might contribute to improving students' behavioral, cognitive, and relational engagement?

CREATING RITUALS FOR ENGAGEMENT

The purpose of classroom rituals is to impose a structure for connecting with our students and having them connect with each other. When we perform a ritual with another person, we communicate that we value them. Commencement rituals, such as developing a special greeting or handshake when students enter the room, communicate to students that they are welcome and belong. Farewell rituals communicate that students will be missed. Celebrations of birthdays and special accomplishments are examples of rituals that recognize the unique life experiences and talents of students in the class. Quarrel rituals, which teach students how to make amends, communicate that conflict has meaning and purpose, that feelings can change, and that dialogue is necessary (Bailey, 2000). Rituals teach children and adolescents that we can educate other people about how we want to be treated.

It is important to remember that rituals don't have to require a huge investment in time. Individual and class accomplishments can be recognized with an *I noticed* ritual during morning meetings, with a group high-five, or on an announcement board. Moreover, we often connect important rituals in our lives with food. But many districts have increasing restrictions on food or snacks in the classroom. It is important to remember that children and adolescents don't necessarily need food to be a part of the rituals. In Montessori schools, one of the beloved rituals children look forward to is the walk around the sun that children complete on their birthdays. Teachers have the class sit in a circle with a picture of the sun in the center. The class sings "Happy Birthday" and then the child who is celebrating holds a globe in his or her hand and walks around the sun one time for each year since they were born. Summer birthdays are celebrated at the beginning and the end of the year to ensure each child is acknowledged.

> Consider your own classroom:
> What rituals do you *already* have in place?
> What additional rituals might contribute to improving students' behavioral, cognitive, and relational engagement?

PLANNING TO PROMOTE COGNITIVE ENGAGEMENT: CLASSROOM GOAL STRUCTURES

Marilyn Watson and Victor Battistich (2006a, 2006b) have been studying classroom communities for over 30 years. Their research has identified several impediments to building engaging, caring classroom communities.

Time. Building a classroom community where all students share in the responsibility for classroom management and are engaged in learning activities takes time.

Conflict and Orderliness. Many teachers come to the profession with the intuitive notion that quiet, orderly, and calm classrooms are ones where students are learning. Not necessarily. Years of research on cooperative grouping indicate there can be an energizing, constructive value to conflict. "Intellectual conflict is not only highly desirable but also an essential instructional tool that energizes student effort to learn" (Johnson & Johnson, 2009, p. 37). Conflict, whether it is a conflict of interest experienced between the teacher and a student or two students, controversy in two belief systems, or an internal conceptual conflict a student experiences when he or she meets with new ideas, presents an opportunity to teach students new skills.

Competition. United States culture has long held individualism, competition, and survival of the fittest as fundamental values. And yet in the classroom we find competition undermines teachers' abilities to promote optimal engagement and learning for all children and adolescents.

School Practices and Inertia. Our schools continue to endorse remnants of old practices we know do not work. In order for teachers to build caring communities, they need smaller classes, longer periods, time to plan, time to develop relationships, and schoolwide management plans. Schools take longer to change than classrooms, and teachers can experience a sense of inertia—that their efforts to make changes in their classroom are undermined by the school culture. It can be hard to persevere when faced with another budget crunch. Often, creative scheduling and teamwork are needed to create opportunities to have meaningful connections with our students.

Societal Mobility. At the heart of relational models of classroom management is a teacher's ability to cultivate a close caring relationship with and among students. As more families move within and between cities, this task becomes more complex. It becomes essential for teachers to integrate routine *getting to know you* rituals into their instructional design.

Beliefs About Students. One consistent finding in the relational management literature is that, "if teachers have a negative view of children, or of particular groups of children, they will be unable to trust their students enough to have high expectations for them or to view their behavior in a positive light" (Watson & Battistich, 2006a, p. 270).

While routines and rituals will contribute to promoting students' behavioral and relational engagement in the classroom, to promote optimal cognitive engagement in the classroom, we need to critically evaluate the types of implicit and explicit messages we send students about the purpose of engaging in learning activities. In the 1960s, Robert Rosenthal (see Rosenthal & Jacobsen, 1968) began examining expectancy beliefs and self-fulfilling prophecies, research that has remained robust into the early 2000s. When teachers expect students to perform, regardless of skill level, they behave in different ways that bring about the expected performance. Self-fulfilling prophecies, such as those about student ability, operate through two forms of messages we send to our students— explicit messages (i.e., what we consciously *try* to say) and implicit messages (i.e., what we unconsciously said). Like Rosenthal, Barbara Finkelstein (2001) argues that when we keep our expectations for socially responsible behavior high, children and adolescents will live up to them. For example, in her study of how adolescence has been defined over time, she learned that when we expected adolescents to go through a period of unconstructive rebellion they often conformed to our expectations—engaging in unproductive and risky behaviors. However, in the 1960s–1970s, meaningful, constructive rebellion from high school and college students was behind many of the civil rights changes the nation experienced.

In 1973, Rosenthal "derived four major types of teacher behaviors that appear to be associated with [teacher] expectancy effects" (as cited in Hall et al., 2001, p. 163). These include the following:

1. *Climate.* Consider your interactions with each student. To what extent are you warm and encouraging to each student?

2. *Feedback.* Consider the amount and quality of the feedback you give to each student. To what extent do you offer enough (too much, too little) evaluative comments on each student's ongoing performance? To what extent do you balance corrective instructional feedback with focused praise of student work?

3. *Input.* Consider how you allocate your effort and time across students. To what extent does your effort to try to teach the child match his/her needs?

4. *Output.* Consider the number of learning opportunities presented to each child. To what extent does each child have enough opportunities to participate and respond?

> Think back to Alice's and Kim's classrooms.
> What kinds of expectations about behavior and learning was each teacher communicating to her students?
> To what extent were they holding high expectations for socially responsible behavior?

In this chapter, we focused on how to evaluate the different organizational and structural features of our management design. It is important to remember that the design of our learning activities also communicates these same expectations about how hard we are trying to reach each student, how many opportunities we are creating for students' success, and the reasons why students should engage in our learning tasks. In the following chapters, we elaborate more on the types of verbal and nonverbal messages teachers send to their students that contribute to creating a classroom climate that supports behavioral, cognitive, and relational engagement as well as relationships that model caring for ourselves, for each other, and for our work.

CONNECT TO YOUR PRACTICE

Reflect on the Current State of Your Classroom Management Practices

Improving the climate and organization of the classroom begins with a candid reflection of the current state of the classroom (adapted from Frieberg & Stein, 1999).

Step 1: Start with your senses and ask yourself: How does my classroom look, smell, feel, and taste? (i.e., what do students eat in the classroom as part of instructional activities or snacks? For secondary teachers, these responses might vary by the periods they teach. Are students more likely to be hungry during certain periods?)

Ask yourself: What led me to organize my classroom to look, smell, feel and taste like this?

Step 2: Create a mission statement for your classroom. Close your eyes and envision the type of students you want to have in your classroom by the end of the year. What kinds of skills (academic and social) can they enact? What kinds of motivations drive them to engage in your class? What kinds of relationships do they exhibit with you and the other students in the class?

Step 3: What groups or individuals need to be involved in your classroom in order to bring about your mission statement?

Step 4: What initial structural and organizational changes can you make that would have the highest impact and could be accomplished in the shortest period of time? At the midpoint of the year? Near the end of the year?

EXPLORE STUDENTS' PERSPECTIVES

Evaluate Student Drawings

Several scholars have documented the power of indirectly assessing the climate of a classroom by asking your students to draw a picture (Frieberg & Stein, 1999; Murphy, Delli, & Edwards, 2004) or construct a metaphor (Oldfather, West, White, & Wilmarth, 1999). Projective measures, where we present students with an ambiguous task under the assumption that they will project their attitudes on the task, are appropriate for both young children (prek–2nd grade) who may have limited reading comprehension and adolescents. Prompts for students might include

- Draw a picture of how you see our classroom.
- Draw a picture of an effective (a good) teacher. If you teach a specific content area, you might modify this to include the content area (i.e., a good science teacher).
- Draw a picture of our classroom community.
- [For middle grades and older] Identify a metaphor for our classroom (i.e., Our classroom is like a deep sea submersible.) Draw a picture of your metaphor and label the comparisons you are making in the metaphor.

When analyzing the pictures, evaluate the essence of the whole picture. Begin by looking at each image independently. What meaning was each student trying to convey? You may want to consider if students are carrying different beliefs or stereotypes about teaching or about the content area that you teach into the class.

Next, you may want to attend to issues of proportion, perspective, and the method of instruction the child chose to portray. This might include the size and placement of the teacher relative to the students. Is the teacher portrayed as big and influential relative to the students? Is he or she portrayed as being close or distant to students—central to the activity of the classroom or on the periphery?

Finally, you may want to note any omissions, inclusions, and erasures that are unique to a particular students' drawing. Do some images seem different or unique compared to the rest of the class?

Once you have attempted to understand each student's image, try making a master list of the attributes you noted for the images. Do some attributes appear more often than others?

What can you conclude about the types of impressions most students have about the classroom from these drawings? How does this make you feel?

Were you able to identify a subset of students who appear to have less adaptive perceptions of the classroom from these drawings? How does this make you feel?

KEY TERMS

Class commitments: A set of statements that outline the purposes and roles of each member of the classroom. Students and teacher(s) commit to these statements daily.

Class norms (rules/procedures): The behavioral expectations and generally expected procedures in a classroom; they can be defined and enforced by the teacher or can be defined and enforced cooperatively by the teacher and all students.

Consistency management: The decisions a teacher makes in his/her instructional planning to maximize student engagement.

Distributed leadership: An approach to management by which students are assigned shared classroom responsibilities based on their individual talents and areas of interest.

Routines and rituals: Consistent procedures and practices in a classroom that help minimize disruption by helping students feel safe, connected, and in control.

Seams in instruction: Times and spaces in a classroom, such as during transitions, when students often exert their independence or autonomy. The seams are greater when students are physically transitioning between activities or classrooms. During these times, teachers need to be thoughtful about how they manage their own and their students' movement.

RESOURCES FOR TEACHERS

Frieberg, H. J., & Stein, T. A. (1999). Measuring, improving, and sustaining healthy learning environments. In H. J. Frieberg (Ed.), *School climate: Measuring, improving, and sustaining healthy learning environments* (pp. 11–29). London, UK: Routledge Falmer.

Manke, M. P. (1997). *Classroom power relations: Understanding student-teacher interaction.* Mahwah, NJ: Lawrence Erlbaum.

McCaslin, M., & Good, T. (1992). Compliant cognition: The misalliance of management and instructional goals in current school reform. *Educational Researcher, 21*(3), 4–17.

Murphy, P. K., Delli, L. A., & Edwards, M. N. (2004). The good teacher and good teaching: Comparing beliefs of second-grade students, preservice teachers, and inservice teachers. *Journal of Experimental Education, 72,* 69–92.

U.S. Department of Education. (2008, September). *Reducing behavior problems in the elementary school classroom: IES practice guide.* Washington, DC: Institute for Education Sciences, National Center of Education Evaluation and Regional Assistance. Report is available at http://ies .ed.gov/ncee/wwc/publications/practiceguides/

3

How Do I Create a Classroom Climate That Supports Engagement?

Classroom climate has often been thought of in terms of the extent to which different dimensions of the classroom shape the quality of the interactions between and among students and teachers. Discussions of climate can be challenging because climate is often described as the "feel" of a classroom. Does a classroom feel warm and inviting or cold and distant? But classroom climates can be more complex than a simple temperature; they can describe the common types of feelings and motivations students have for academic work.

> Consider Alice's and Kim's classrooms.
> How does Lauren compare and contrast the climate
> or feel of each classroom?

We often forget that teachers, like parents, act as socializing agents. They can influence the quality of students' social and intellectual experiences through their abilities to create classroom contexts and climates that stimulate students' inherent motivation and instill values of being motivated to learn (Brophy, 2000; Oldfather & Dahl, 1994). A consistent finding in the motivation research literature is that classrooms tend to have one of two foci: a **learning orientation** or a **work orientation**.

The teachers who promoted a *learning orientation* introduced activities with emphasis on what students would learn from them, encouraged students to work collaboratively and help one another, and treated errors as natural parts of the learning process and stimulants for follow-up instruction. In contrast, the teacher who promoted a *work orientation* spoke primarily in terms of task completion rather than learning. She stressed completing the work within stated time limits when introducing activities, emphasized competition rather than cooperation among students, and gave the correct answers following errors but did not use the errors as occasions for helping students to overcome their difficulties in learning. (Brophy, 2000, p. 26)

In a classroom oriented toward learning, the climate tends to have a more open, collaborative feel because students are focused on understanding. In a classroom oriented toward completing work, the climate tends to feel more burdensome with students focused on labor and production. It is important to understand that research consistently demonstrates that when students approach classroom tasks with a learning orientation, their understanding and performance of the task improves. This is because students with a learning orientation are focused on understanding and mastering the tasks we give them. When they are focused on understanding academic tasks, they are more likely to expend effort, understand inconsistencies, and persist in the face of difficulties.

We often indirectly communicate our beliefs about the value of academic work through our instructional design. When designing individual learning tasks, teachers need to think about being on *TARGETT*. TARGETT is an acronym for seven dimensions of learning activities that communicate to students our beliefs about the purpose of classroom work. Each of these dimensions contributes to the feel of the classroom.

Tasks. What is your rationale for having students accomplish each task? Research indicates that students will be naturally engaged in tasks that are meaningful and authentic. The kind of work we ask students to engage in communicates to them our beliefs about the value of school work to prepare them to be engaged citizens. To what extent do the tasks you assign have personal relevance to the students? Do the tasks help students to understand kinds of labor they may do as adults?

Autonomy. What choices can you offer students? Research indicates that students will be more engaged when they are presented with opportunities to control their own learning. The amount of autonomy we offer to students communicates to them our beliefs about their ability to make sound choices about their learning outcomes and control their own learning behaviors. To what extent do students have autonomy in choosing how they will complete their work and in determining the products of their work?

Recognition. How will you recognize student work? Research indicates that competition, which can erode engagement, can increase when only a few students are routinely recognized. It is important to think about the implications of public versus private recognition and the extent to which *all* students in the class have an opportunity to be recognized for academic excellence. How do you currently recognize students publicly and privately? Do all students have an opportunity to be publicly recognized for academic excellence?

Grouping. What opportunities do students have to work together? How will you differentiate instruction? Findings consistently show students are more engaged when they are provided opportunities to work together; however, the seams for group work can also provide opportunities for students to be off-task more often (see also Chapter 5). Additionally, children are astute observers of classroom dynamics; they quickly become aware when the level of challenge systematically varies across work groups. Research consistently suggests that it is important to avoid always grouping lower achievers together. What strategies do you currently employ for designing cooperative learning groups? To what extent do you find students are behaviorally, relationally, and cognitively engaged during group work? How might the other dimensions of tasks, autonomy, recognition, evaluation, and time contribute to students' abilities to work collaboratively and productively in groups?

Evaluation. How will students participate in the evaluation process? Research consistently shows that when students are provided opportunities to participate in peer- and self-evaluation of assignments, their mastery of content increases. To what extent do you currently engage students in reflecting on their own and their peers' strategies and performance?

Time. How will you manage instructional time? Research suggests that students are more likely to adopt a work orientation when students feel rushed to learn. Consider how you feel about the curricula you teach. Do you currently feel rushed to move through content? What strategies have you, or your colleagues, used in the past to manage your own feeling of being rushed to teach?

Teacher Socialization of Enthusiasm. Finally, Jere Brophy emphasized the importance of monitoring the explicit messages we send students about our own excitement for learning activities. His research suggests that enthusiasm for learning can be infectious, with students reporting feeling more engaged in academic tasks they perceive their teachers to be passionate about. Consider each unit you teach. How do you feel about the content? How can you communicate your excitement for learning about each unit?

DEVELOPING STUDENTS' AUTONOMY AND RESPONSIBILITY: CLASSROOM DISCOURSE PATTERNS

More challenging to change than our instructional and management designs are the content and patterns of communications we have with students. Classrooms are inherently communicative environments (Morine-Derschimer, 2006). Similar to our management and instructional design, this happens because our patterns of oral and written participation in the classroom communicate to students our values about who belongs and who can be successful in our class. As teachers, we hold a lot of power in the classroom, and the messages we send to students are imbued with that power. Communications between teachers and students are largely asymmetrical. Through their public and private communications with teachers, students learn about their teachers' beliefs about how and when it is appropriate to talk to them, to other adults, and to their peers in the classroom. "Even when rules and routines are *explicitly* developed, discourse studies suggest that they become 'invisible' to participants after extended regular use" (pp. 129–130). For this reason, **classroom discourse** is often viewed as a mediator of students' learning and achievement. That is, some types of classroom discourse have been found to promote students' learning whereas others have been found to diminish learning. Researchers who study classroom discourse patterns seek to understand how students use classroom discourse to make sense of their learning tasks, how the private communications that happen between students align with or resist teachers' curricular goals, and how we can understand students' reluctance (or overt resistance) to participate.

The feel, or climate, of our classroom, will not only be affected by the decisions we make about our instructional design but also by the patterns of public and private communication we have with our students. Identifying the underlying discourses in our classroom can take a great deal of time and reflection because these discourses reflect the overarching ethos of our classroom. Below, however, are several discourses that have been consistently found to promote students' learning and achievement.

Do I Speak to My Students in a Way That Promotes Their Autonomy and Develops Their Sense of Responsibility?

Stefanou, Perencevich, DiCintio, and Turner (2004; see also Reeve, 2006) argued teachers may actually exert *more* influence in their classrooms when they learn to *cede* behavioral and intellectual autonomy to their students. This may sound counterintuitive, but remember students have a fundamental need to feel autonomous. When they don't, they may seek out inappropriate ways to exert their control. As mentioned earlier, by offering them meaningful choices, teachers can simultaneously meet our needs for order and predictability in the classroom without compromising students' needs. The challenge, however, is not simply to plan for student autonomy in the classroom but to monitor the messages we send about whether we really want students to be responsible for their own behavior. Johnmarshall Reeve and colleagues have studied the behaviors of controlling and **noncontrolling teachers**. They argue that noncontrolling teachers speak to their students in fundamentally different ways than controlling teachers. "When teachers rely on informational, noncontrolling language, they communicate classroom opportunities and requirements through messages that are informational and flexible rather than controlling and rigid" (Reeve, 2006, p. 229).

> To respond to displays of lackluster motivation or poor performance, a controlling teacher will generally treat poor performance evaluatively . . . (e.g., "Work faster; you should've been done by now"). In contrast, autonomy-supportive teachers treat students' poor performances as problems to be solved, and they communicate classroom requirements through a language that is informational and flexible. The goal is to help students better to diagnose the underlying cause of their poor performance and take the action needed to address the problem . . . "I've noticed that you chose not to join the group's work; is anything wrong?" (Reeve, 2006, p. 229–230)

Stefanou and colleagues (2004) argued that we need to monitor our messages about autonomy and responsibility on three different channels in the classroom: behavioral autonomy, procedural autonomy, and cognitive autonomy. When students are engaging in counterproductive behaviors, teachers can redirect by asking, "Can I give you some responsible choices for how to respond?" When students are expressing resistance to the tasks we assign, we can redirect by asking, "Can I give you some suggestions about how to get started/ work on/complete this task?" When students are struggling to understand the content or complete the tasks they have chosen, we can redirect by asking, "Can I give you some teacher ideas?" (Bailey, 2000). Finally, Reeve (2006) argued that noncontrolling teachers use gentle discipline techniques that involve explaining why one way of thinking or behaving is appropriate and another is not and that guide students toward making more responsible choices. The opposite of gentle discipline techniques "is power assertion, which is a controlling socialization strategy that involves forceful commands and an insistence that students comply with the teacher's request or demand" (Reeve, 2006, p. 233).

When I Speak to My Students, Am I Clear About How to Be Successful?

The literature is consistent that teachers who have **clear expectations** for academic behaviors and tasks tend to have students who feel more autonomous. As teachers, it is important for us to clarify the rules, routines, and rituals for our classrooms as well as share with students the *reasons* that underlie classroom norms and activities. It may be helpful to find out if students are familiar with the rules, routines, and rituals for our classrooms. If not, we need to provide students with time to understand and practice appropriate patterns of interaction. This can be particularly important when it comes to collaborative behaviors such as partnering and group work. Rules, routines, and rituals should be posted clearly as cues for student behavior. When presenting academic tasks, we need to define, clarify, and model the various learning activities we expect students to engage in. Because the reasons that underlie classroom norms and activities become invisible to students after extended regular use, we may need to build in opportunities to revisit these rationales.

When I Speak to My Students, Am I Clear That Everyone Belongs?

Students have a fundamental need to feel connected to their teachers and peers. Research consistently shows that they monitor the underlying **discourse of inclusion**: Are all students wanted and valued in this classroom? It is important to work to provide *all* students with extensive opportunities to learn and be successful. Students will notice when we use procedures that promote wide participation among students;— procedures that identify and capitalize on the individual expertise each student brings to the classroom. Research consistently indicates that students are more engaged and learn more in classrooms that value and establish explicit **norms of cooperative collaboration**. This includes teaching students strategies and processes for resolving differences in opinions and beliefs. Discourse theorists remind us that we need to monitor both the public and private talk of students since students actively monitor both channels of communication. They argue that teachers can benefit from listening unobtrusively to conversations of students while working in groups to understand the social world they are constructing (Morine-Derschimer, 2006).

When We Are Having a Conflict, Do I Communicate the Value of Reconciliation?

Fundamentally, discourse theorists remind us to be alert to ways our communicative behavior during what we might think of as nonacademic interactions may constrain the instructional discourse. They remind us that to develop an accepting climate in which students are encouraged to solve problems and behave responsibly, we need to model how to respond to conflict and disagreement. This involves accepting and acknowledging when students express unpleasant emotions about the tasks they are asked to do (e.g., "This is boring." "This is stupid."). When we acknowledge students' emotions, we ask them to be responsible for their emotions, and we create an opportunity to model the appropriate expression of these emotions as well as how to solve the problem of being disinterested with an activity. We need to monitor **killer statements** that silence conversations in the classroom. Killer statements can reflect direct assertions of teacher power (e.g., "You need to get back on task.") or they can reflect indirect assertions of student power (i.e., disparaging or critical comments made to silence you or another student in the class). When conflict arises, model and promote the use of active listening strategies. Seek to identify the thoughts and feelings you and your students are having about the conflict.

Work toward a resolution that meets both the students' needs to feel competent, autonomous, and connected in the classroom and your instructional and managerial needs.

> Consider Alice's and Kim's classrooms.
> What might the discourse patterns
> Lauren observed be communicating to students
> about who belongs in the class, how to be
> successful, and how to solve problems?

CONNECT TO YOUR PRACTICE

Evaluate Your Teacher Talk

Record a typical instructional period. Choose an instructional period that begins with students transitioning into the classroom and ends with their transition out of the classroom. Self-evaluate the key ideas in this chapter by choosing two or more types of teacher talk to self-analyze.

Type	Communication	What I Said	What I Should Have Said
Goals	Learning-oriented messages		
	Work-oriented messages		
Autonomy	Autonomy supportive		
	Autonomy nonsupportive		

(Continued)

(Continued)

Control		
Noncontrolling statements		
Controlling statements		
Power		
Inclusive messages		
Killer statements		

Reflect on what you learned from this analysis by creating an action plan for changing classroom climate through how you communicate with students. Consider how changing your instructional design (TARGETT) might contribute to more adaptive communication patterns.

KEY TERMS

Autonomy supportive: A classroom environment that supports the development of student autonomy by giving students more opportunities to make their own decisions and choices.

Classroom climate: Aspects of a classroom environment that communicate its goals, power structure, and orientation to learning, social relationships, and emotions.

Classroom discourse: The spoken and unspoken communication that exists in a classroom between teachers and students and can hold underlying messages for students about the teacher's beliefs and expectations.

Classroom goal structure: The types of cognitive, behavioral, social, and emotional goals teachers set for students in their classrooms.

Clear (teacher) expectations: When teachers are conscious and transparent about their beliefs about the way students are to behave in the classroom. This might include expectations about homework, classwork, peer relationships, conflict, and solving problems.

Discourse of inclusion: Messages teachers send to students about their value and acceptability in the classroom; these messages can be sent implicitly or explicitly through verbal or nonverbal communication.

Killer statements: Statements of power that silence the sharing of emotions and expression in a classroom.

Learning orientation: A classroom that is focused on learning; this orientation is communicated to students by the scaffolding of tasks, an emphasis on collaboration, and a general acceptance of mistakes as opportunities to learn problem solving.

Noncontrolling teachers: Teachers who seek to guide students' thinking and behavior through conversation, explanation, and gentle discipline.

Norms of cooperative collaboration: The general expectations and procedures in the classroom that dictate how students interact with each other and solve interpersonal conflicts.

Work orientation: A classroom that is focused on work; this orientation is communicated to students by the structuring of tasks, encouragement of competition, imposition of time limits, and correction of errors.

RESOURCES FOR TEACHERS

Ames, C. (1990). Motivation: What teachers need to know. *Teachers College Record, 91,* 409–421.

McCombs, B. (n.d.). Developing responsible and autonomous learners: A key to motivating students [Teacher module]. Retrieved from http://www.apa.org/education/k12/learners.aspx

Oldfather, P., West, J., White, J., & Wilmarth, J. (1999). Learning through children's eyes: Social constructivism and the desire to learn. *Psychology in the classroom: A series in applied educational psychology.* Washington, DC: American Psychological Association.

Reeve, J. (2006). Teachers as facilitators: What autonomy supportive teachers do and why their students benefit. *Elementary School Journal, 106,* 225–236.

Rohrkemper, M., & Corno, L. (1988). Success and failure on classroom tasks: Adaptive learning and classroom teaching. *Elementary School Journal, 88,* 296–312.

Wells, M. C. (1996). *Literacies lost: When students move from a progressive middle school to a traditional high school.* New York, NY: Teachers College Press.

PART II

Management as a Function of Classroom Relationships

4

How Do I Model Caring in Relationships With Students?

OBSERVING BELIEFS ABOUT RELATIONSHIPS

Scott

Scott was the choral teacher for Finn County schools. At the time of our interview, he was in his fifth year teaching at both the middle school and high school. He had taught elementary school for two years prior. He held undergraduate and graduate degrees in music education and had taught private music lessons for 15 years. At this point in his career, Scott was struggling to understand why he continued to experience conflict with some students despite his deep commitment to developing relationships and how hard he worked at trying to connect with each of the students in his class.

> It's high energy, a lot of emotion, a lot of out-of-your-seat standing and doing different activities. . . . If I am trying to teach a particular concept, I might have them do a particular motion to get that across. . . . I like to keep the class real

free. . . . I don't want to be too tight, too formal, so it's very humorous at times. There's also discipline there. I don't want that to sound like a contradictory statement, but the students learn that there are particular times in the classroom here that they need to be well focused, and so they do that.

When giving corrective feedback, I try to make it a personal responsibility that you [the student] need to learn to know when this behavior is appropriate and when it is not. If it continues, I might pull a child aside and speak with that child individually and just, you know, be more direct with them. . . . Discipline is not necessarily something you do to a child. It's a form of encouragement not to repeat the behavior. Discipline in the sense that they have self-discipline; that they have a desire to achieve a goal and they are willing to work hard for it.

A good relationship is an open relationship. It's one where they feel they can come to me and talk about things that are going on in their lives. Or if they have a real problem, a real concern, they can come and ask my advice. The whole idea that you must treat every child the same is just for the birds. It's not fair, not that life is fair. . . . But I just try to explain to them the most unfair thing I can do is treat you just like everyone else because you're different; you were created differently, you have different abilities and different needs, and so if you can focus on those things and try to make a child feel important, I think that makes them want to learn.

When asked about why he thought relationships were important for learning, Scott began:

If a child and a teacher have a good relationship, that opens the door for learning. If a child has a positive relationship with me there is more active listening to what I am saying to watching what I am doing, and they are more apt to learn because [they know] I want to teach them. . . . But, I think even more important than the facts we teach them is the decision making process that we teach them. And, if I can help them do that, it's a life skill.

My students choose to be here . . . every child in my classroom. And, therefore, some of the discipline things that other teachers might have to deal with, I don't have to deal with. I also have the option that if a child does have a discipline problem, they can be moved to another exploratory class because my classes are limited in size. There's only one choir class and there's twelve hundred students. I can't possibly teach every child and so the classes are auditioned and the children are selected and I then have a waiting list of children who want to be in the class. . . . Students either love me or hate me. Those that love me stay with my program and those that don't like me tend to get out of the program very quickly. There are just some people, and I think just that their personalities don't fit. . . . I dread having a child who is closed to my class or a child whose parents forced them to be in the class. . . . I use the metaphor of the glove and hand: there are just some matches that don't fit. You should try your best to make that glove fit. There are gonna be some very difficult and trying students and usually that is a sign that something is wrong, that a child needs something special. So if you can take the time to adjust then the glove begins to fit better.

My philosophy of teaching? Connect with the students. If I can get them to enjoy what they're doing, they will learn it. . . . We spend a lot of time with each other and I really get to know my students. And, I can teach my students more than one year. I have the potential of teaching them three years in middle and then four years in high school because of both of my positions. And we also do a lot of field trips. When you spend that much time with a child outside of the school setting, you begin to build rapport with them and they start coming to you. . . . I think middle school kids are challenging because they are changing and they are coming into themselves. They are becoming adults and yet they are still children. They're very unique in that respect and I think if you can treat them uniquely, not as an adult, not as a child, but somewhere in the middle. I think number one is to treat them as individuals. . . . There is nothing wrong with losing a child to another class. That happens. I don't think it's a negative thing for either person as long as it doesn't go on too long. You have to catch it early.

Faith

At the time of our interview, Faith was an 18-year veteran teacher of the Finn County schools. She had previously taught fifth and sixth grades in elementary school but had spent the last 12 years teaching primarily sixth grade at FCMS, since it opened. At the time of our interview, Faith was teaching a combined seventh and eighth grade language arts and science to the SUCCESS class and was, largely, moving up with many of the sixth graders she had taught previously.

> My students are primarily lower level as far as ability goes. They need some extra help that they don't qualify for special education or Chapter or any of those other places. But they are not considered behavior problems or any of those things and most of them tend to be on the low socioeconomic end too.

At the time of our interview, Faith was struggling with where to draw boundaries with her students when she felt like she was working too hard to make the relationship work.

> My philosophy of teaching. They need to stay busy, that's for sure, to eliminate problems. I mean they need to be doing things, you know, that they feel are meaningful to them. They definitely need to have respect for the teacher and that's not always easy. But if they are treated with respect, they respect back. It's not a big philosophy, I guess. Get in there and teach those objectives, you know. . . . This year, we can start right in with something new and not spend those first weeks trying to get a grip on each other and trying to figure each other out.
>
> There's nothing typical about middle school kids. . . . You know a big range of what you can encounter. I don't expect kids to just sit there and not say anything. I like when they are willing to talk 'cause, you know, sometimes they're funny and all those [inappropriate] things sort of endear you to them. . . . A good relationship is when they'll talk to you about their problems. They'll come to you when they're having a problem; that they are not afraid, you know, of either physical—like being yelled at—or embarrassed. That they feel all open relationships. . . . It'll mean they'll ask for help. They trust you; they know you are helping them. They know they're respected; that they trust me enough to come ask me something. It's not like I have all these skills going on, but those are the things that I think are ideal.
>
> Bad relationships are when they don't trust you to ask for help or tell you when they do not understand. It's a bad relationship when they're changing classes so fast and they just slip through and you never get to know them. Every year, there are a lot of kids that you feel more drawn to than others, and you know, the

others you have to try to make yourself concentrate more on [them]. Some are more personable. They just jump out at you and then there is that little kid that just never opens their mouth and you just overlook them if you're not careful. You know they can just kind of slip through the cracks. You just have to try to get to them. I dread the kind of student that's going to be late for class and then come up to you and want to go somewhere and then get mad at you when you say no. You know, the kind of kid that just has their mind made up already and you feel pretty sure that you're not going to be able to get them no matter what you're going to do. I dread that. They worry me, you know. I just want to do something about them but I realize I probably can't. . . . You know, sometimes the dreaded student, they'll come back years later and they've just matured and everything is going fine. It wasn't as hopeless as you thought.

How do you build credibility with your kids? You don't go back on your word. You have to live up to your promises and if you can't you have to explain why. You have to give them feedback: good, bad, whatever. Some kids are harder to get along with because they've had bad experiences before and they just expect things to go bad for them. There are just a lot of them that are angry already. They've had too many failures, or they just got off on the wrong foot. They expect another year of the same old thing and they just come in with the same attitude they've had and everything just goes downhill from there. . . . Grading? Give them results back fast so that they know what's going on with them. Grade fairly and you have to have [sound] reasons for everything. I've taught on five-teacher teams, and we'll all sit down and discuss our kids, and all five of us will have a different take on the kids. Sometimes a kid that has been driving everyone nuts, one teacher will say, "Oh, he doesn't give me any trouble." . . . Sometimes a teacher can just take one under her wing that's had problems and turn them around.

Note: Cases were reconstructed from Davis (2001a); see also Davis (2006).

In Chapter 1, we approached classroom management from the perspective of need fulfillment. Specifically, we explained that students are optimally motivated to engage in classroom activities when they perceive their three basic needs to feel autonomous, competent, *and* related are met. And conversely, students may disrupt learning when basic needs are not met. Arguably, the most critical source of relatedness in any classroom is the relationship a student develops with his or her teacher. Cultivating relationships with students is complex. The two teachers in the cases above were identified by their administrator for their exceptional abilities to cultivate relationships with some of the most difficult students in the school. And yet they held very different beliefs about how to develop teacher-child relationships. Arguably, relationships with students can be challenging. We don't always have it all figured out.

> Scott and Faith are both struggling to understand their difficulties in connecting with students.
>
> What struggles do you share in common with Scott and Faith? Are there struggles you experience that they don't address?

For 30 years, a growing body of literature has documented the importance of students' perceptions of teacher relationships on their classroom motivation, learning, performance and school completion (Connell & Wellborn, 1991; Daniels & Clarkson, 2010; Davis, 2003; Lambert & McCombs, 1998; Skinner & Belmont, 1993). In a recent meta-analysis, Cornelius-White (2008) found students' perceptions of caring teacher relationships accounted for as much as 30% of the variability in academic and social outcomes. Caring relationships significantly predict students' participation, satisfaction, self-efficacy, critical thinking, standardized achievement in math and language, increasing attendance, reducing disruptive behavior, and higher grades. The research is very clear; students who perceive their teachers as caring tend to engage more with the content, take intellectual risks including probing when they do not understand, and persist in the face of failure.

There are several hazards to the literature on caring teachers. One pitfall is that we can fall into the trap of classifying teachers as either caring or not caring, forgetting that most teachers pursue teaching as their career because they want to connect with and serve children and adolescents. The second pitfall is the belief that it is simply impossible for teachers to connect with and care for all of the students in their classes. In both of these perspectives, caring is treated as a feeling, an emotion that teachers or students feel for each other that is either present or absent in a relationship. In contrast, scholars Nel Noddings (1988) and Lisa Goldstein (1999) conceptualize caring as a process—that is, something teachers do rather than something they feel. They argue that caring is an ethic, or a moral value, that we communicate to our students through our selection of curriculum, our lesson planning, the norms we establish, and our individual interactions with students. When we begin to think about caring as a process, we can then evaluate how *what* and *how* we choose to teach communicates to our students what we care about.

For example, the standards we establish in our classroom communicate to our students the values we care about (see Chapter 2). And the frequency and quality of our interactions with individual students communicates who we care about. Caring is not an entity that exists or does not exist in a classroom. Teachers exhibit caring about content, values, and relationships in different ways. The absence of caring teacher behaviors sends powerful messages that impact students' motivation and learning. The beauty of a process perspective is that caring configurations in classrooms can and should be somewhat idiosyncratic depending on the age of students we teach, the content we teach, and the way we personalize our instruction.

TEACHER BELIEFS ABOUT RELATIONSHIPS

As with beliefs about classroom management and discipline, what it means to be caring is also likely to involve more generalized beliefs about the nature of classroom relationships. In our own work (Andrzejewski & Davis, 2008; Davis, 2006; Newberry & Davis, 2008), we've found teachers appear to struggle to resolve two tensions when selecting students as relationship partners.

> How do I balance my responsibility for instruction
> and academic outcomes with the responsibility for
> developing relationships with students?
>
> How do I balance the time and effort
> needed to develop relationships with
> a few uninviting students with the time and
> effort needed to accomplish my relational and
> academic goals for the class?

The teachers in our studies tended to make instructional decisions, and in some cases disciplinary referrals, depending on whether they assumed responsibility for supporting or improving lower achieving students, or whether they saw the remediation of school under-preparedness as the responsibility of outside agents (e.g., Title I or Chapter I teachers). Indeed, several studies have documented that teachers make decisions about who to connect with by weighing individual students' assets and obstacles (see also Muller, Katz, & Dance, 1999). These assets might include the perception of a student's similarity, attractiveness, social skills, and a child's expressed desire for a relationship. These assets all contribute to getting picked from what Roland Tharpe and his colleagues (Tharpe, Estrada, Dalton, & Yamauchi, 2000, p. 56) call the "limited pool of eligible relationships" in the classroom. Similarly, some of the teachers in our studies appeared to approach relationships with students from a cost-benefit perspective. In other words, they were cautious about investing costly time, energy, and emotions into a relationship with a student who might not reciprocate (Davis, 2006; Davis, Chang, Andrzejewski, & Poirier, 2010; Newberry & Davis, 2008). And unfortunately, when teachers approach relationships with students from a cost-benefit perspective, the research consistently finds the students who may *need* relationships with their teachers the most may be the *least* likely to be selected as relationship partners (Baker, Grant, & Morlock, 2008; Davis & Lease, 2007). Conversely, Lisa Delpit (1995) argued that when teachers committed to establishing and maintaining relationships with uninviting students, their commitment had a transformative effect on students' attitudes and achievement patterns.

> Close your eyes and remember
> two students, one boy and one girl, with whom
> you felt you developed a close, productive
> relationship. What factors contributed to these
> successful relationships?
>
> Now remember two students, one boy and one girl,
> from whom you spent the year feeling alienated.
> What factors contributed to these distant and
> unproductive relationships?

Why are some teachers more willing to commit to building relationships with and care for those uninviting students? Knee, Patrick, and Lonsbary (2003) argued that over the course of their lifetime, adults develop intuitive theories about why relationships succeed and fail. Specifically, their research shows that some people hold **growth beliefs** of relationships, whereas others hold **destiny beliefs** of relationships. Individuals with destiny beliefs about relationships tend to believe that some people are fated to meet, be lifelong friends, fall in love, and so forth. Relational conflict, differences of opinion, or value and arguments tend to be viewed as a sign of inherent incompatibility. Teachers who hold destiny beliefs about relationships with students are more likely to view some of the students as either inherently compatible or not. In contrast, individuals who hold growth beliefs about relationships tend to view conflict as a natural byproduct of growth in a relationship. Teachers who hold growth beliefs are more likely to believe that challenges in relationships, including differences, can be overcome. These views of relationships serve as lenses for interpreting all social tasks including selecting relationship partners, perceiving the limitations of one's partner, investing effort, interpreting conflict, and persisting through differences.

> Consider Scott and Faith. How might their
> interactions with their students be influenced by
> their beliefs about interpersonal relationships?

Again, it is important to remember that our beliefs are a form of subjective reality. What we believe to be real and true guides our decision making, behavior, and interactions with students and, in turn, creates an objective reality in our classroom—what our students experience as real and true. We can choose to modify our beliefs and, in doing so, change our approach to our relationships with students. What does it mean to be a caring teacher? To be caring means to critically evaluate about what and for whom you actively care. If we enter relationships with children believing the relationship to be inherently incompatible, we can create a self-fulfilling prophecy.

> How might Scott's and Faith's beliefs about relationships between students and teachers have affected their abilities to connect with each of the students in their classrooms?

WARM DEMANDING TEACHERS

What are the characteristics of teacher relationships that not only promote cooperation in the classroom but also student engagement with the curriculum? A consistent finding across the studies of relationship quality is that the perception of caring by students has a strong instructional component. Teachers perceived as caring delineate intellectual boundaries, including what will be learned and the standards for mastery, which their students find meaningful. Teachers perceived as caring focus a great deal of energy on cultivating their students' interest in the content they are teaching. And to do so they employ a variety of strategies that connect content to their students' lives.

Teachers perceived as caring also set high expectations for all students in their classes and really press their students to understand the material, not merely for the sake of performing on a test but to understand the world around them. Holding high expectations means understanding what students are capable of accomplishing when they are placed in an optimal learning context (i.e., where all their needs as learners are met) and holding ourselves accountable for creating those contexts and opportunities to learn. Among teachers who push their students to excel, what distinguishes teachers perceived as caring is the quality of their interpersonal interactions. Across the literature, caring teachers have been defined as **warm demanders**, an idea conceived by Judith Kleinfeld (1975) and developed by Jacqueline Irvine (1998). Warm demanders exert influence on their students' learning through their relationship. They are not willing to let a child turn in lesser quality work or fail. Instead, with compassion, they express to their students that they believe they can do better and will work with them to improve their work.

> In what ways do Scott and Faith evidence the characteristics of personal warmth and active demand?

Kleinfeld (1975) argued teachers evidencing a warm-demanding approach cultivate a sense of closeness in the classroom by monitoring their physical proximity to their students such as smiling frequently, maintaining a close body distance, and demonstrating a willingness to engage in appropriately touching students, which can be as simple as giving a high five to a student who mastered a challenging task. Behaviors that involve modulating our verbal (i.e., what we say) and nonverbal (i.e., how we say it) messages are called **immediacy behaviors**. Immediacy describes the students' perception of a teacher's physical and psychological closeness (Frymier, 1994). Teachers' deployment of immediacy behaviors tend to predict students' ratings of instructor credibility and their willingness to comply and may contribute to their motivation and achievement (see also Burroughs, 2007).

Cultivating closeness also involves **emotional proximity** behaviors. Julianne Turner and colleagues (Turner et al., 2002;

Turner et al., 1998; Turner, Meyer, Midgley, & Patrick, 2003) found that teachers who were rated by observers and students as expressing pleasant emotions with a greater frequency tended to have students that reported more adaptive patterns of math motivation. Teachers can also cultivate emotional proximity through the use of personal disclosure (Davis, 2006; Davis, Gableman, & Wingfield 2011) such as sharing their own school experiences, how they use what they are learning in their lives, and information about their personal lives. Making decisions about what to share from our personal lives can be difficult (Andrzejewski & Davis, 2008) and often requires us to be conscious and set boundaries around topics that we feel are vulnerable. However, Lannutti and Straumen (2006) documented college instructors who were perceived to engage in greater amounts of self-disclosure tended to receive more positive evaluations from their students.

> Consider how you can systematically use self-disclosure in the classroom.
>
> What can you share about your personal experiences in school? Your experiences learning the material you teach?
>
> What topics do you feel vulnerable discussing?
>
> How can you respond to students in a productive way if they initiate conversations about these topics?

It is important to note, however, that emotional proximity and immediacy behaviors are *vehicles* for communicating caring and creating a sense of closeness but may not necessarily reflect caring in the way Nel Noddings (1988) and Lisa Goldstein (1999) contended. From their perspective, *caring is communicated by the behaviors we engage in to promote students' understanding and participation in the classroom.* Similarly, Kleinfeld (1975) argued that personal warmth, while a *necessary* condition for eliciting a high level of intellectual performance, is not *sufficient*. In her study, sentimentalist teachers who scored high on personal warmth but low on active demand-ingness, appeared to cause more harm to the relationship by alienating minority students from content and school. This is because they were often found to sympathize with students' challenges by allowing them to provide excuses for not com-pleting work or participate in class. Kleinfeld argued that in order to have influence with students, particularly students from different ethnic and/or economic backgrounds, teachers must cultivate the legitimacy of their academic content for students. They must demand more than their students think they are capable of, making their demands clear, and must articulate the implicit cultural assumptions that impede student success.

> If students are to produce what they are capable of, the teacher must demand more than students think they are capable of. . . . Making clear academic demands also involves the difficult task of articulating cultural assump-tions underlying learning tasks in [Western] classrooms. (pp. 327–328).

Again, this connects to Nel Noddings' (1988) assertion that when we care, we dedicate our time and efforts to making sure the students are supported in meeting these high expectations.

Immediacy behaviors, as described earlier, also appear to play an important role in cultivating students' feelings of influ-ence. Van Tartwijk (1993 as cited in Wubbels, Brekelmans, den Brok, & van Tartwijk, 2006) examined the role of teachers' non-verbal immediacy behaviors along five channels: space, body, face, visual behavior, and voice. That means that when students interpret our interactions, they draw from each channel to decode our real meaning. He found one of the challenges begin-ning teachers face is their inability to simultaneously attend to and coordinate two or more nonverbal channels (Kounin, 1970). For example, in order for teachers to appear both warm and demanding, they must modulate both the content (i.e., the message we want to send) and relational aspects of the message (i.e., how we plan to send the message; Wubbels, Creton, & Holvast, 1988). It is the relational aspects of our message that involve modulating how we hold our body, our use of space, our facial expression, and our tone of voice (Wubbels et al., 2006). Thus, developing our sense of immediacy in the classroom is a skill that takes time and practice to cultivate.

Attempts to influence students, however, involve more than simply being thoughtful about the messages we send. Influencing students involves using our authority as teachers to persuade students to try on new thoughts, behaviors, and even emotions. In her recent study of warm demanding teachers, Franita Ware (2006) argued that warm demanders teach with authority but do not abuse their authority (see also Irving & Fraser, 1998; Noblit, 1993). Warm demanders influence students to participate in curricular activities by emphasizing the inherent value of the activity and the ability of students to master increasingly challenging material. Ware argued that warm demanding teachers are a relational authority, not an intellectual authority. Warm demanders seek to understand what each student needs and interpret behavioral and curricular resistance as inherently having meaning. Warm demanding teachers advocate for those who have no voice, and position their curricular and pedagogical decisions from a place of social responsibility (Case, 1997, p. 36) offering feedback that is both affirmative and corrective.

> In what ways do Scott and Faith exemplify the
> qualities of warm demanding teachers?

FEEDBACK, PRAISE, AND ACADEMIC PRESS

In Chapters 1 and 2, we described how traditional models of classroom management seek to influence students through the use of rewards and consequences, often with hidden cost to classroom climate and the development of students' abilities to regulate their own behavior. How can we influence students *without* the use of rewards and consequences? A consistent finding from the field of educational psychology is that our verbal messages, or feedback, to students significantly affects how they feel about themselves and their schoolwork. In a seminal article, Carol Dweck (1999) argued that we often come to teaching with intuitive understandings that children need to receive praise that they are smart or good in order to behave and feel they are intelligent. She described the ways in which teachers' attempts to globally praise students' abilities (e.g., You're so smart!) or achievements (e.g., Good job!) often backfire to produce children who are afraid to take risks in the classroom.

> I had seen over and over that children who had maladaptive achievement patterns were already obsessed with their intelligence—and with proving it to others. The children worried about how smart they looked and feared that failing at some task—even a relatively unimportant one—meant they were dumb. They also worried that having to work hard in order to succeed at a task showed they were dumb. (p. 3)

A consistent finding in the field of educational psychology is that effective praise from teachers and parents relies on describing children's behavior, not judging it. Again, children and adolescents have a fundamental need to connect with the people in their lives. When we notice their efforts and accomplishments, we not only meet their needs for attention but we also act as their mirror (Bailey, 2000) allowing them to modify their behavior to meet their emerging set of standards. For most of us, this can be a really challenging shift because the kinds of praise we have received have been laden with the judgments of others. When students ask us to read their writing/problem solving, it feels natural to offer our opinion. But noticing the behaviors that you want to promote can actually be more effective.

> I notice in this piece how you took the time to really describe each character and the setting. I really felt like I knew them and could picture them in my mind. Now that you have the plot settled, I wonder if in your next read through the piece, you might focus on . . .

> I notice when you solved this problem that you took the time to follow each step we described in class. I can really see how you were working through this problem. Before you turn it in, I wonder if you might take a moment to . . .

Several scholars argue we need to shift from judging children's and adolescent's actions to noticing what they are doing. "Noticing helps children become aware of themselves. This awareness wires the brain for self-control. . . . In contrast, judging helps children become aware of our view of the world, not theirs" (Bailey, 2000, p. 32). Some students, however, do crave explicit positive affirmation. Figure 4.1 outlines 12 guidelines for giving students effective praise—the kind that maintains their focus on the process of learning. In each guideline, we as teachers are pushed to personalize our affirmations, to affirm students' efforts not abilities, their deployment of strategies not simply the accomplishment, and to foster their own self-evaluations of their progress.

> Consider Scott's and Faith's views on discipline and corrective feedback. How do their views align with Dweck's and Bailey's notions of praise and noticing?

| Figure 4.1 | Brophy's Guidelines for Effective and Ineffective Praise |

Effective Praise	Ineffective Praise
1. Is delivered contingently	1. Is delivered randomly or unsystematically
2. Specifies the particulars of the accomplishment	2. Is restricted to global positive reactions
3. Shows spontaneity, variety, and other signs of credibility: suggest clear attention to the student's accomplishment	3. Shows a bland uniformity, which suggests a conditioned response made with minimal attention
4. Rewards attainment of specified performance criteria (which can include effort criteria, however)	4. Rewards mere participation without consideration of performance processes or outcomes
5. Provides information to students about their competence or the value of their accomplishments	5. Provides no information at all or gives students information about their status
6. Orients students toward better appreciation of their own task-related behavior and thinking about problem solving	6. Orients students toward comparing themselves with others and thinking about competing
7. Uses students' own prior accomplishments as the context for describing present accomplishments	7. Uses the accomplishments of peers as the context for describing students' present accomplishments
8. Is given in recognition of noteworthy effort or success at difficult (for *this* student) tasks	8. Is given without regard to the effort expended or the meaning of the accomplishment (for this student)
9. Attributes success to effort and ability, implying that similar successes can be expected in the future	9. Attributes success to ability alone or to external factors such as luck or easy task
10. Fosters endogenous attributions (students believe that they expend effort on the task because they enjoy the task and/or want to develop task-relevant skills)	10. Fosters exogenous attributions (students believe that they expend effort on the task for external reason—to please the teacher, win a competition or rewards, etc.)
11. Focuses students' attention on their own task-relevant behavior	11. Focuses students' attention on the teacher as an external authority figure who is manipulating them
12. Fosters appreciation of and desirable attributions about task-relevant behavior after the process is completed	12. Intrudes into the ongoing process, distracting attention from task-relevant behavior

Source: Brophy (1981)

Middleton and Blumenfeld (2000; see also Middleton & Midgley, 2002) argued that having a **learning orientation** in the classroom may not be enough. "In other words, students may be getting the positive motivational message that the reason they do their work is to improve and master the material, but in those motivating situations they are not experiencing any different level of demand for learning and understanding" (p. 375). They describe the ways in which students perceived their teachers to individually press them toward accomplishing different goals. They identified three types of **academic presses**: (a) **press for understanding**, (b) **press for performance**, and (c) **press for competition**. They use the term *press* to not only describe a type of intensity in the relationship, but depending on the kind of press, it can connote the quality of perceived interactions between students and their teachers.

Presses toward performance and competition, however, can undermine both teacher and peer relationships in the classroom. In focusing on trying to complete work, students may receive messages from their teachers that they are competing with the other students in the class to be recognized for the best products. Or they may receive messages from their teachers that following directions and procedures and completing work on time is more important than understanding the material. Relationships with teachers can erode if students perceive a shift in the focus of teachers' attention away from the students in the classroom and onto the products of the classroom. And relationships among peers can erode when students perceive they are competing with each other for their teachers' attention or recognition. This is because the locus of caring shifts from caring about *you* and caring about *our* work to caring about a *few* and caring about *their* work.

However, when teachers press their students for understanding, they implicitly communicate to students their confidence in students' abilities to master content and their perception that students can be successful pursuing that type of career. The focus is on caring about student learning and caring about our work together. Pressing students toward understanding can represent a type of differentiation of instruction or cognitive scaffolding that entails "focusing student attention, checking understanding, drawing out reasoning, and making connections" (Middleton & Blumenfeld, 2000, p. 386). When pressing students toward mastering meaningful academic tasks, students receive supportive, task-specific feedback that they can be successful at the task. For example, when students appear to master a task quickly, a teacher might press them to make connections with other units they have completed or identify how the content is relevant to their lives.

> What kinds of press do you observe from Scott and Faith? How might these different types of presses affect their interactions with students?

CONNECT TO YOUR PRACTICE

Reflect on Your Implicit Beliefs About Relationships

Knee and colleagues (2003) argue that over the course of their lifetime, adults develop intuitive theories about why relationships succeed and fail. They have developed a publicly available survey that they have been using to understand how individuals approach personal relationships.

Consider this a preassessment, allowing you to identify your initial orientation toward personal relationships. Respond honestly to each item. Then use the scoring rubric at the end to calculate scores for each dimension.

What do the scores tell you about your beliefs about successes and failures in relationships? Where might these beliefs have originated? How do you see these beliefs enacted in your current classroom management practices? Your interactions with students?

Figure 4.2	Preassessment for Identifying Your Initial Orientation Toward Personal Relationships

Relationships succeed and fail for a variety of reasons. Look at the statements below and decide on a scale of 1= never true to 5 = always true the extent to which the statement reflects your belief about the nature of relationships (Knee et al., 2003).

	Never true			Always true
1. Potential relationship partners are either compatible or they are not..	1	2	3	4	5
2. The ideal relationship develops gradually over time......................	1	2	3	4	5
3. A successful relationship is mostly a matter of finding a compatible partner right from the start...........................	1	2	3	4	5
4. A successful relationship evolves through hard work and resolution of incompatibilities................................	1	2	3	4	5
5. Potential relationship partners are either destined to get along or they are not................	1	2	3	4	5
6. A successful relationship is mostly a matter of learning to resolve conflicts with a partner............................	1	2	3	4	5
7. Relationships that do not start off well inevitably fail........................	1	2	3	4	5
8. Challenges and obstacles in a relationship can make love even stronger........................	1	2	3	4	5
9. If a potential relationship is not meant to be, it will become apparent very soon........................	1	2	3	4	5
10. Problems in a relationship can bring partners closer together.............	1	2	3	4	5
11. The success of a potential relationship is destined from the very beginning........................	1	2	3	4	5
12. Relationships often fail because people do not try hard enough...........	1	2	3	4	5
13. To last, a relationship must seem right from the start........................	1	2	3	4	5
14. With enough effort, almost any relationship can work........................	1	2	3	4	5
15. A relationship that does not get off to a perfect start will never work..	1	2	3	4	5
16. It takes a lot of time and effort to cultivate a good relationship................	1	2	3	4	5
17. Struggles at the beginning of a relationship are a sure sign that the relationship will fail........................	1	2	3	4	5
18. Without conflict from time to time, relationships cannot improve.........	1	2	3	4	5
19. Unsuccessful relationships were never meant to be............................	1	2	3	4	5
20. Arguments often enable a relationship to improve............................	1	2	3	4	5
21. Early troubles in a relationship signify a poor match between partners........................	1	2	3	4	5
22. Successful relationships require regular maintenance...................	1	2	3	4	5

(Continued)

Figure 4.2 (Continued)

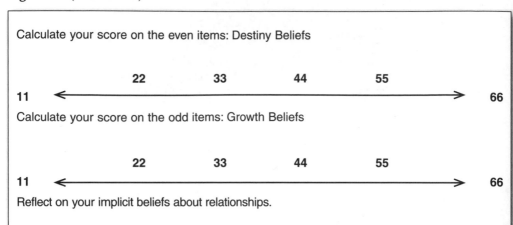

Calculate your score on the even items: Destiny Beliefs

Calculate your score on the odd items: Growth Beliefs

Reflect on your implicit beliefs about relationships.

Do your intuitive beliefs about classroom management lean more toward growth or destiny?

How do you see these beliefs enacted in your current classroom?

KEY TERMS

Academic press/teacher influence: Efforts by teachers to push students toward certain goals or achievements.

Destiny beliefs: The belief that relationships are predestined and that conflict therefore indicates incompatibility; destiny beliefs lead to abandoning of difficult relationships.

Emotional proximity: Behaviors exhibited by warm demanding teachers that cultivate emotional closeness to students by expressing emotions and sharing personal experiences.

Growth beliefs: The belief that relationships are built over time and that conflict is therefore a natural event that can be overcome; growth beliefs lead to persevering through difficult periods in a relationship.

Immediacy behaviors/teacher proximity: Behaviors exhibited by warm demanding teachers that involve creating physical closeness to students through positive body language, standing close to students, and using touch appropriately.

Learning orientation: A classroom that is focused on learning; this orientation is communicated to students by the scaffolding of tasks, an emphasis on collaboration, and a general acceptance of mistakes as opportunities to learn problem solving.

Press for competition: Teachers' recognition of or attention to a few students with the best performance or products.

Press for performance: Teachers' messages that the outcomes of work are more important than the process of learning.

Press for understanding: Teachers' messages that they believe students can learn; it helps push students to understand the content being taught.

Teacher autonomy support: A teacher's attempts to help students become autonomous and successful in school by making their own decisions and choices about their education; sometimes teachers must scaffold their autonomy support so that students learn to make choices that propel them toward success rather than making choices that allow them to disengage.

Teacher expectations: Teachers who hold high expectations for students recognize that as teachers, they are responsible for creating optimal learning environments in which all students can achieve their maximum potential.

Teacher immediacy behaviors: Verbal and nonverbal behaviors, such as smiling and physical touch, that teachers use to develop physical and psychological closeness with their students.

Warm demanding teachers: Teachers who use their relationships with students to exert influence on their students' performances.

RESOURCES FOR TEACHERS

Bondy, E., & Ross, D. (2009). The teacher as warm demander. In M. Scherer (Ed.), *Engaging the whole child: Reflections on best practices in learning, teaching, and leadership* (pp. 55–63). Alexandria, VA: Association for Supervision and Curriculum Development.

Brophy, J., & McCaslin, M. (1992). Teachers' reports of how they perceive and cope with problem students. *Elementary School Journal, 93*, 3.

Chang, M., & Davis, H. A. (2009). Understanding the role of teacher appraisals in shaping the dynamics of their relationships with students: Deconstructing teachers' judgments of disruptive behavior/students. In P. Schutz & M. Zembylas (Eds.), *Advances in teacher emotion research: The impact on teachers' lives* (pp. 95–127). New York: Springer.

Daniels, D. H., & Clarkson, P. K. (2010). *A developmental approach to educating young children: Classroom Insights from Educational Psychology Series*. Thousand Oaks, CA: Corwin.

Davis, H. A. (in press). Teacher-student relationships. In J. Hattie & E. Anderman (Eds.), *International handbook of student achievement*.

Davis, H. A. (2009). Caring teachers. In E. Anderman & L. Anderman (Eds.), *Psychology of classroom learning: An encyclopedia (PCL)* (Vol. 1, pp. 138–141). New York, NY: Macmillan Reference.

Dweck, C. (1999, Spring). Caution: Praise can be dangerous. *American Educator*, pp. 4–9.

Jones, V., & Jones, L. (2007). *Comprehensive classroom management: Creating communities of support and problem solving* (8th ed.). Boston, MA: Allyn & Bacon.

Rimm-Kaufman, S. (n.d.). *Improving students' relationships with teachers to provide essential supports for learning* [Teacher module]. Retrieved from http://www.apa.org/education/k12/relationships.aspx

Weinstein, C. (1998). "I want to be nice, but I have to be mean": Exploring prospective teachers' conceptions of caring and order. *Teaching and Teacher Education, 14*, 153–163.

5

How Can I Build Supportive Peer Relationships?

REVISITING ALICE'S AND KIM'S CLASSROOMS

Lauren

In the introduction, we introduced you to Alice and Kim. Alice took a relational approach to classroom management. But she had a group of students who had a lot of conflict with each other. Kim took a traditional approach to classroom management and had what appeared to be a well-behaved group of students. If an uneducated observer were to enter both Alice's and Kim's classrooms, he or she might be inclined to label Alice's classroom as a poor learning environment and Kim's as an excellent learning environment. Alice's classroom would likely appear loud, disorganized, perhaps even chaotic, whereas Kim's would seem calm and orderly.

One week I observed a **cooperative learning** activity in both classrooms. Kim gave the directions three times. Some students appeared to understand the directions the first time. Other students did not appear to understand the directions even after the third repetition. Once the students broke into small groups, one or two students took control of the learning activity, performed the expected task, and then all students in the group recorded their answers independently. There was no discussion, no expression of thoughts or ideas, and no visible excitement among students. Yet there was also no conflict.

Alice gave directions once. Just as in Kim's classroom, some students appeared to understand the directions and others did not. Some groups took several minutes to get started on the cooperative learning activity, and others got right to work. The students in Alice's classroom were visibly animated about the task. They engaged in constant discussion, both about the learning activity and about their personal lives. They all appeared to share in the responsibility for the assignment. Conflict among group members erupted several times during the lesson. Some students argued about the task: What were they supposed to do? How were they supposed to do it? Other students argued about the content: Whose ideas were most worthy of inclusion? Whose ideas were correct? Others argued about materials: Who had the brown marker? Which way was the paper turned? Whose turn was it to write? Each time Alice attended to the group quickly, but in lieu of solving the group's problem, she served only as a facilitator. She asked the students questions that prompted them to consider the task and their own needs as well as the needs of their group members.

> How might the quality of students' learning in Kim's and Alice's classes reflect the quality of their relationships with their peers?

Most teachers would agree that peer relationships in the classroom are crucial for child development and learning, particularly when those relationships are supportive. Research shows that students who have support from their academically successful peers have higher levels of academic engagement (Kinderman, 1993) and academic performance (Kurdek & Sinclair, 2000; Wentzel & Caldwell, 1997) and increased performance over time (Ryan, 2001). Similarly, students who report having friends at school also tend to be more sociable, cooperative, and less aggressive than students who do not have reciprocated friendships (Wentzel, Barry, & Caldwell, 2004).

Most teachers are also aware of the potentially adverse effects of unsupportive peer relationships. Students are often disruptive if they are seen acting out, particularly when a student or group of students are behaving in ways that oppose academic classroom goals or **bullying** in the classroom—behavioral problems that are typically addressed with behavioral solutions (Tingstrom, Sterling-Turner, & Wilczynski, 2006). In this chapter, we offer some suggestions for teachers who want to build a supportive community of peers in their classroom using strategies geared toward positive relational engagement. We begin by offering insight into the benefits of allocating time to developing an **inclusive peer culture** and offering some strategies for building positive communities in the classroom, and we conclude by addressing some of the issues teachers face when relationships become problematic.

Why Are Peer Relationships Important?

Most students have peer-oriented **social goals**. Moreover, they typically pursue these goals simultaneously with their academic goals (Wentzel, 1991b). Social goals, like academic goals, are useful in explaining why students make the choices they do based on needs and/or desires in an academic context. One way that teachers can develop positive peer relationships by satisfying social and academic goals is by developing an experience of community in their classrooms.

Forming good relationships with peers is an important part of students' development. Learning to accept and be accepted by one's peers involves different skills than those involved in forming friendships. Our chapter focuses on improving the overall quality of peer relationships in the classroom, as opposed to friendships, because the literature suggests teachers have much more influence over the quality of peer relationships in their classroom and **peer acceptance**. Peer acceptance generally refers to how much an individual is liked or disliked by his or her peers. Whereas peer acceptance can have a positive influence on students' social and academic development (Birch & Ladd, 1997), the experience of **peer rejection** can lead students to hold negative perceptions of school and to exhibit greater school avoidance (Ladd, 1990) and poorer school adjustment compared to accepted peers (Coie & Dodge, 1988; Crick & Ladd, 1990).

BUILDING A POSITIVE CLASSROOM COMMUNITY

Earlier in Chapter 3, we introduced you to the concept of classroom climate—the feel of a classroom as a place that supports understanding, responsibility, and an orientation toward conflict resolution. But classrooms can also be thought of as **communities of learners**: established by instructional methods, guided by the instructor, and developed over time by members of the classroom (Summers, 2006). All classrooms are communities, but stressing the fact that community in the classroom is important does not make it the foundation of classroom management (Watson & Battistich, 2006a). In order for a classroom to be a community in the relational sense, members must feel emotionally connected to one another, have a voice and role in the activities of the community, and feel that their needs are being met in the community (McMillan & Chavis, 1986). When communities fulfill these conditions their members experience a sense of belonging and trust that their needs will be met through mutual commitment (McMillan & Chavis, 1986; Osterman, 2000).

> In what ways do Kim's and Alice's classrooms embody a community of learners?

There are two programs that we highlight because they focus on the kind of relational engagement we describe in Chapter 1 and offer specific suggestions on how to manage classrooms by building classroom community: the Child Development Project (CDP; Battistich, Watson, Solomon, Lewis, & Schaps 1999) and the open classroom (OC) learning community (Rogoff, Turkanis, & Bartlett, 2001). The CDP is an elementary school program with the goal of integrating a focus on children's social and moral development in which community is the foundation of classroom management and caring relationships (Watson & Battistich, 2006a, 2006b). The OC learning community is a community of learners program in which the primary goal is deep learning that leads to higher order thinking (Rogoff, Bartlett, & Turkanis, 2001).

THE CHILD DEVELOPMENT PROJECT

The Child Development project (CDP) is a comprehensive elementary school program designed to enhance children's prosocial development, where prosocial development is defined as the development of attitudes and motives that reflect sincere concern for the rights and needs of others as well as the self (Battistich, Elias, & Branden-Muller, 1992). The CDP program consists of an intensive classroom component that consists of four major elements:

1. *Developmental discipline*: By involving students in class rule setting and decision making, teachers are able to build positive interpersonal relationships in the classroom via mutual problem solving techniques (see Chapter 2).

2. *Cooperative activities*: By designing learning activities that encourage students to be fair, considerate, and socially responsible, teachers are able to provide opportunities to reflect on how these values and skills can be applied to both academic and nonacademic tasks.

3. *Activities to enhance interpersonal understanding and prosocial values*: By using relevant literature, class meetings, and discussions, teachers are able to enhance

students' sensitivity to feelings, needs, and perspectives of others.

4. *Opportunities for prosocial action:* Students take responsibility for doing classroom chores, helping other students in class, and performing community service activities.

Findings from extensive research on the CDP by Battistich and his colleagues (Battistich & Horn, 1997; Battistich, Schaps, & Wilson, 2004; Solomon, Watson, Delucchi, Schaps, & Battistich, 1988) found that the program has positive effects on students' social competencies, acceptance by peers, and social adjustment. Overall, the program was effective in creating a caring and supportive environment in the classroom. Students' sense of community was strongly associated with the use of cooperative learning—we believe that utilizing cooperative learning in the classroom can help students build a sense of community, particularly if teachers are able to emphasize the four components mentioned above.

> Consider the ways in which Alice and Kim organize cooperative learning activities. In what ways do their activities encourage students to be fair, considerate, and socially responsible, and improve interpersonal understanding?

THE OPEN CLASSROOM LEARNING COMMUNITY

The open classroom (OC) learning community is a parent-cooperative elementary school in Salt Lake City that was developed with the "community of learners" philosophy, where both children and adults engage in learning activities in a collaborative way (Rogoff, Turkanis, & Bartlett, 2001). From this overarching principle are other principled features of learning as a community:

1. *Purposeful learning with a clear goal, building on the children's interests, needs, and prior understanding*: By creating interesting learning activities and helping students understand why they are learning, teachers are able to help students thrive in their classroom learning environment.

2. *Assessing progress while aiding learning*: Assessment is an ongoing, formative process that follows the students through conversations about their learning.

3. *Taking responsibility and making choices.* By having a dialogue about their choices and the consequences that result, both the students and the teacher gain insight into this important aspect of learning.

4. *Making decisions and learning as a community*: Learning through collaboration is central to learning as a community, which is learned through involvement and shared thinking of students and teachers.

Like the CDP, cooperative learning in the OC model plays a major part in developing a sense of classroom community among peers. However, Rogoff, Turkanis, & Bartlett (2001) are quick to point out that simply adding the technique of having children work in "co-operative learning" teams is quite different than a system in which collaboration is inherent to the structure:

Co-operative learning sessions in U.S. schools are often brief and insulated from the overall structure of the classroom, where for much of the day, only the teacher is supposed to speak; if children speak, it is one at a time and only to the teacher. The exceptional times, when children tutor each other or work in co-operative groups, do not correspond to a community of learners, which is itself coherently structured as a collaborative system. (Rogoff, Turkanis, & Bartlett, 2001, p. 13)

Like the OC learning community, we support cooperative learning practices for achieving a sense of community *if* it is an integral part of classroom culture and practice. When cooperative learning is successful as a pedagogical and community building strategy, students develop positive cooperative abilities and inclinations, altruistic behavior, interpersonal understanding, feelings of belonging, and acceptance of others (Johnson & Johnson, 1989; Johnson, Johnson, & Maruyama, 1983; Sharan, 1990; Slavin, 1990).

> Consider the culture in your classroom surrounding cooperative learning activities. To what extent are students required to participate as a member of a community, responsible for their choices and for the members of their group?

BUILDING COMMUNITY USING COOPERATIVE LEARNING

Cooperative learning is defined broadly as the instructional use of small groups so that students work together to maximize their own and each other's learning (Webb, 1989). In their extant research on cooperative learning, Johnson and Johnson (1989) have established that successful cooperative learning occurs when individuals share common goals. While Johnson and Johnson's model assumes process-based interaction among students during cooperative learning, their research has concentrated on student products or outcomes of good cooperative learning design in three broad categories: effort to achieve, positive interpersonal relationships, and psychological health.

It is the quality of relationships outcome that we believe is closely related to literature citing students' need for community or belongingness in the classroom (Summers & Svinicki, 2007). Specifically, Johnson and Johnson (2003) claim that cooperative efforts can result in mutual liking and respect among peers. Johnson and Johnson have even gone so far as to recommend that "schools have to focus on building (1) a learning community, (2) positive relationships among heterogeneous students, and (3) positive relationships between classmates and lonely, isolated, alienated, at-risk students" (Johnson & Johnson, 1998, p. 18). A study among grade-school students confirmed that cooperative learning situations promoted more positive interpersonal relationships than conditions that utilized interpersonal competition or individualistic learning (Johnson, Johnson, & Maruyama, 1983).

In what contexts does cooperative learning support classroom community and positive social relationships? We believe the most relevant strategies stem from creating a shared social context and can include methods such as **reciprocal teaching, collaborative problem solving,** and the use of cognitive tools and intellectual roles (Palinscar & Herrenkohl, 1999). Reciprocal teaching is very useful in the promotion of text understanding, and it involves the teacher and students taking turns leading discussions about shared texts. In this type of instructional approach, thinking is made public and students have the opportunity to hear others' perspectives on the text. In a study of collaborative problem solving in science (Palinscar, Anderson, & David, 1993), students were coached in the use of explanations as they engaged in problem solving and were asked throughout instruction to describe their experience in terms of how they

1. contributed to the group's effort,

2. identified activities that involved sharing resources and taking turns,

3. worked to understand others' ideas, and

4. built on one another's ideas.

Finally, in a study of the use of *cognitive tools and intellectual roles* in fourth-grade science (Herrenkohl & Guerra, 1998), students were taught in small groups how to formulate explanations to an audience, thus assuming responsibility for questioning and discussion in the context of whole-class discussions. More ideas for collaborative learning are found in varying texts for instruction (e.g., Frey, 2011; Gillies, 2007).

PEER RELATIONSHIP ISSUES IN THE CLASSROOM

Cooperative learning may not be the best, or only, solution for students who have emotional or behavioral problems in class. In fact, some researchers have found that children who are uninviting of relationships or who struggle to manage their own behavior may hinder the working of the cooperative groups. In these situations, teachers may need additional training to develop classroom communities in these contexts (Cowie, Smith, Boulton, & Laver, 1994). Two of the most common classroom management concerns surrounding peer relationships are (a) general disruptive conduct where a student with a disability "acts out" in class (e.g., trying to seek negative attention or exhibiting inappropriate behavior toward others) and (b) more directive behavior toward peers like bullying. For some students, teaching them self-regulation skills may be the key to getting students to behave in class (see Chapter 7). For others, like children who have diagnosed behavioral or emotional problems, it may be more difficult to help them develop positive peer relationships because part of the problem is that they have difficulty self-regulating. We argue here that, in addition to teaching students how to self-regulate their behavior, it is also important to teach children how to care for one another as part of the general classroom community in order to achieve relational engagement.

FACILITATING SUPPORTIVE RELATIONSHIPS WITH CHILDREN WITH SPECIAL NEEDS

For many teachers, providing an inclusive environment for all of their students is challenging, and cooperative learning may not be the best, or only, solution.

Inclusive education involves educating students with disabilities in age-appropriate general education classes in which they are perceived as valued members of the class and receive the supports and services they need to succeed. The goals of inclusive education are to facilitate acceptance, belonging, and tolerance among students with and without disabilities. (Soodak & McCarthy, 2006, p. X)

Without a planned intervention, the mere proximity of disabled students with non-disabled students may not be enough to yield classroom involvement, or curtail isolation and rejection (Guralnick, 1999). Many of the programs that are designed to promote acceptance and friendship in inclusive settings are successful if the teacher is an active mediator of these relationships.

In one study that encouraged elementary school teachers to make the rule, "You can't say, 'You can't play,'" based on the book by Vivian Paley (1992), students were focused on ensuring that every member of the classroom be accepted. The intervention was effective at increased participation from disabled students but only if teachers made the rule an integral part of teaching, learning, and social activities in their classroom (Sapon-Shevin, Dobbelaere, Corrigan, Goodman, & Mastin, 1998).

> Consider the norms established in your classroom. To what extent do they emphasize the inclusion of all students?

Finally, it has been suggested that teachers can try using collaborative learning activities for students with disabilities to enhance positive social interactions, particularly for students with Attention Deficit Hyperactivity Disorder (ADHD; Saunders & Chambers, 1996). In a recent study by Watkins and Wentzel (2008), boys with ADHD were paired with a non-disabled peer, who was trained to use elaborative explanations and validating expressions or actions on a cooperative task. In addition to positive changes in planning strategies and planning efficiency, boys with ADHD also improved the quality of their social interactions with peers. We believe that cooperative learning in particular is an excellent method of improving peer interactions and relational engagement in the classroom, particularly if the teacher is concerned with the inclusion of students with disabilities. (See Chapter 7 for a case study of a student with ADHD.)

> Consider the benefits students without disabilities might experience from positive interactions with peers with disabilities.

REDUCING PEER VICTIMIZATION AND BULLYING

Bullying is defined as long-standing, negative behavior conducted by an individual or a group and directed against a person who is not able to defend herself or himself in the situation (Olweus, 1997; Rigby, 1997). A study by Roland and Galloway (2002) demonstrated a strong relationship between teachers' management of the class, the social structure of the class, and bullying, indicating that bullying can be addressed at the classroom level, as opposed to or in conjunction with a schoolwide intervention strategy. While there is some debate over the most effective methods of bullying intervention, researchers generally agree that teachers and peers in the classroom can play a major role in the intervention process (Smith, Anniadou, & Cowie, 2003). For example, peer support methods that support bullying-intervention strategies include collective decision making processes and discussions. For example, in the no blame approach, peers are asked to help exert positive social influence on the bullies so that they will be encouraged to do the right thing by the victim, rather than blaming either the victim or the bully for an act of bullying (Maines & Robinson, 1992).

CONNECT TO YOUR PRACTICE

Explore the Quality of Peer Relationships in Your Classroom

In addition to some of the suggestions we have provided to help students develop a sense of classroom community, it may also be helpful for teachers to gauge the social climate of their classrooms before trying a new instructional method. For example, the Peer Relations Questionnaire (Rigby & Slee, 1993) is a useful tool for uncovering any possible negative relationships, including bullying, among students before planning group instruction (see Figure 5.1).

To analyze the data you collect, begin by adding up the total score for each scale. Items belonging to the scales are these:

Bully Scale: 9, 11, 16, 17

Victim Scale: 3, 8, 18, 19

Prosocial Scale: 5, 10, 15, 20

First, consider each student's individual scores on the survey. If students score 10 or higher on the bully or victim scale, you may have a bully/victim dynamic in your classroom or school that is worth investigating further. If students score lower than 10 on the Prosocial Scale, you may want to emphasize the benefits of helping others and/or civic involvement in your instruction.

Now consider the average scores for your class. In general, are students oriented toward working together in a prosocial way? In general, do students perceive bullying/victimization as a problem in your classroom and/or school? Consider sharing the data you collect with a school counselor to talk about ways to build stronger peer relationships in your classroom. Or consider designing a class project to develop an anti-bullying campaign for your school (for an example, see the Cypress Ranch High School anti-bullying lip dub "Who Do U Think U Are?" at http://bit.ly/LGNEsE).

Figure 5.1	The Peer Relations Questionnaire (PRQ) for Children

Show how often the following statements are true for you. To do this, circle one of the answers underneath each statement.

Never = 1

Once in a while = 2

Pretty often = 3

Very often = 4

	Never	Once in a while	Pretty often	Very often
1. I like playing sports.........................	1	2	3	4
2. I get good marks in class...............	1	2	3	4
3. I get called names by others...........	1	2	3	4
5. I like to make friends......................	1	2	3	4
6. I play up in class............................	1	2	3	4
7. I feel I can't trust others	1	2	3	4
8. I get picked on by others................	1	2	3	4
9. I am part of a group that goes round teasing others.....................	1	2	3	4
10. I like to help people who are being harassed...	1	2	3	4
11. I like to make others scared of me....	1	2	3	4
13. I get into fights at school................	1	2	3	4
15. I share things with others...............	1	2	3	4
16. I enjoy upsetting wimps..................	1	2	3	4
17. I like to get into a fight with someone I can easily beat...............................	1	2	3	4
18. Others make fun of me...................	1	2	3	4
19. I get hit and pushed......................	1	2	3	4
20. I enjoy helping others...................	1	2	3	4

Source: Rigby & Slee (1993)

CONNECT TO YOUR PRACTICE

Evaluate the Quality of Collaborative Learning and Sense of Community in Your Classroom

Once cooperative learning groups are in place, teachers may wish to assess students' perceptions of community and group processing (Summers, Beretvas, Svinicki, & Gorin, 2005). Although this instrument was designed for use with college students, the scales have been modified here to be appropriate for middle school age children and up (see Figure 5.2).

Add up the total score for each scale:

Classroom Community. Students who score 20 or higher have a moderate to strong sense of community or belongingness in the classroom.

Group Processing Evaluation. Students who score 30 or higher have a moderate to strong belief that the group worked well together.

Group Processing Effect on Individual. Students who score 20 or higher have a moderate to strong belief that they personally benefited from group work.

To analyze the data you collect, begin by adding up a total score for each scale.

First, consider the average score, on each scale, across your entire class. In general, do students feel a strong sense of classroom community? Do they tend to perceive that their group worked well together and that they individually benefited from working together *as a group*? Low scores on the classroom community scale could signify that, in addition to structuring group activities, you may need to work on developing a sense of community in the classroom. Consider having a class discussion about what it means to be a "community of learners" and how they affect each other's learning.

Low scores on the group evaluation at the beginning of the year could indicate that students may not have developed the skills they need to collaborate and learn with peers. It might also indicate that the activity or group time require more structuring. Consider using this scale multiple times throughout the year as a way to promote students' reflection on group learning and to refine how you design and structure cooperative learning activities.

(Continued)

(Continued)

Next, consider each student's individual scores on the survey. See if you can identify students who could serve as group leaders because of their positive beliefs or perceptions about group learning. Also see if you can identify students who may need additional support during group time because responses to the group evaluations were so poor.

Figure 5.2 Evaluating Collaborative Learning and Community

The following questions ask you about your feelings and experiences as they relate to group work **in this class**. Please rate the statements as to how strongly you agree or disagree with each statement using the following scale:

Strongly disagree = 1

Moderately disagree = 2

Slightly disagree = 3

Neutral = 4

Slightly agree = 5

Moderately agree = 6

Strongly agree = 7

Classroom Community	Strongly disagree		←	→		Strongly agree	
1. I feel connected to people in this class................................	1	2	3	4	5	6	7
2. I've made friends in this class........	1	2	3	4	5	6	7
3. I feel I fit into this class..................	1	2	3	4	5	6	7
4. I know other people well in this class................................	1	2	3	4	5	6	7

Group Processing Evaluation

1. Overall, each of the group members contributed his or her fair share..................................	1	2	3	4	5	6	7
2. Overall, my group worked well together..................................	1	2	3	4	5	6	7
3. Typically, my group understood what we were supposed to do.......	1	2	3	4	5	6	7
4. Overall, my group members responded positively to each others' questions............................	1	2	3	4	5	6	7
5. Typically, most group members shared their own ideas during group work.....................................	1	2	3	4	5	6	7
6. My group was successful in finishing most of the tasks...............	1	2	3	4	5	6	7

(Continued)

Figure 5.2 (Continued)

	Strongly disagree	←——————→				Strongly agree
Group Processing—Effect on Individual						
1. At this point in the school year, I have a positive attitude about group work...............................	1 2	3	4	5	6	7
2. I value my group as a resource for learning...	1 2	3	4	5	6	7
3. As a result of group work I improved my group-building skills..	1 2	3	4	5	6	7
4. As a result of group work I improved my problem-solving skills..	1 2	3	4	5	6	7

Source: Summers et al. (2005)

KEY TERMS

Bullying: When one student or group of students repeatedly acts negatively toward a student who cannot defend himself.

Collaborative problem solving: An instructional strategy in which one of the teacher's expectations is that students explain how they worked collaboratively on the task.

Communities of learners: Classrooms in which students feel autonomous, connected to each other, and that their needs are respected and met.

Cooperative learning: Opportunities for students to work together in small groups in ways that allow them to share their strengths and build on each other's learning.

Inclusive peer culture: A classroom environment in which all students feel connected to and supported by their peers.

Peer acceptance: Occurs when a student is generally well liked by his or her peers; has a positive influence on the student's academic and social development.

Peer rejection: Occurs when a student is generally disliked by his or her peers; has a negative influence on the student's academic and social development.

Reciprocal teaching: An instructional strategy in which the teacher and students take turns leading discussions.

Social goals: Students' goals regarding their social relationships with their peers; often students actively pursue these goals throughout the school day alongside their academic goals.

RESOURCES FOR TEACHERS

American Psychological Association's Bullying Module: http://www.apa
    .org/topics/bullying/index.aspx
U.S. Government Website on Bullying: http://www.stopbullying.gov/

Cooperative Learning Websites

It Gets Better Project: http://www.itgetsbetter.org/

Johnson and Johnson: http://www.cehd.umn.edu/research/highlights/coop-learning/

Salt Lake City Open Classroom Philosophy Website: http://ocslc.org/index.php/philosophy/

Slavin: http://www.tolerance.org/tdsi/author/robert-slavin

6

How Do I Connect With Diverse Students?

OBSERVING DISCOURSES ABOUT DIVERSITY

Lauren

One year I had an African American girl named Amiyah in my second-grade classroom. I was immediately drawn to Amiyah, who was a vibrant, smart, funny girl, but I never felt that I got her. As a student, she had a lot of qualities that fit with my expectations for students. She was helpful; when I asked the class to help me remember a thought or an idea I wanted to save for later, I could count on Amiyah to be the first one to remind me. She had an incredible sense of humor, and even at 7 years old, she knew how to lighten a tense mood with a well-timed joke. Amiyah was also spirited. She would try anything I asked of the class with incredible flexibility and enthusiasm. In other ways though, Amiyah frustrated me. While she was intelligent and capable, she often played, looked around the room, or daydreamed rather than completing her work. Sometimes, her humor caused disruptions to other students' learning. And her self-isolating friendship with a class-mate named Dameon often led to mischief.

After months of trying to understand and fix Amiyah's problems, I had an *aha* moment. In January, we had our first round of standardized testing. The morning of the first test, Amiyah fell apart. She doodled all over the test packet, refused to read the reading passages, and bubbled in answers as a pattern. She disobeyed stringent testing rules by exclaiming, "I hate this test!" and by purposefully falling out of her chair, nearly causing the proctor to declare a misadministration of the test. After testing was over, I pulled Amiyah aside and scolded her about her behavior during the test. She immediately crossed her arms and began to scowl, and I prepared myself for an angry outburst. But much to my surprise, Amiyah began to sob, and words began to spill out of her mouth. Slowly, her story unraveled: The night before the test, she reminded her mother that she was supposed to go to bed early because of the test, but they ended up staying out late at her cousin's birthday party. Once she finally got to bed, she couldn't sleep because her little brother was kicking her all night. I learned that Amiyah was responsible for getting her siblings ready for preschool. But that morning, she couldn't wake them up on time, and her mom yelled at her for missing the bus. Though I'd been teaching Amiyah for months, I knew very little about her life outside of school. I was completely unaware of how the priorities of her family differed from the ones we set at school, how different her family was structured compared to my own, and how much responsibility she had caring for her siblings. Why was I trying so hard to force my values and expectations on Amiyah? Why did I believe there was only one way to be a good student? How did Amiyah's home life intersect with her school life to form her education? Why was I trying to fix her?

We (Heather, Jessica, and Lauren) are White, middle-class women. For most of our lives, we took for granted the larger discourses that framed our interactions with students who came from different backgrounds than our own: **discourses of meritocracy, deficit thinking, color blindness**, and **choice**. A **discourse** is an implicit way of thinking about the world that we often take for granted as true. We collect discourses from our everyday interactions with our world because they manifest in our political, legal, and economic structures. When we are unaware of them, we allow them to guide our behavior and they work to maintain the status quo—a status quo where minority, low-income, and nonnative-speaking children underperform their middle-class, White peers.

A **discourse of meritocracy** leads us to believe that only the deserving are rewarded with good grades, high-paying jobs, and happiness in life. But this discourse ignores all the ways in which our society is structured to marginalize groups of people, particularly children from low-income homes, and keep them from fully participating in society. It fails to recognize the innocence and inherent goodness of all children as deserving. A **discourse of deficit thinking** leads us to believe that anyone who is different from the "American Ideal" lacks the essential qualities they need to be successful in life. But this discourse ignores our rich history of multiculturalism and the ways in which democracy is enhanced by diversity of thought, value, and skill. A **discourse of color blindness** leads us to believe that race, ethnicity, religion, and sexual orientation don't matter—that when we see race, we will necessarily behave in ways that are exclusionary. But this discourse ignores the long history we have in this country of creating legal, political, and social structures that exclude people of different races, ethnicities, religions, and sexual orientations from full participation, full inclusion in society. And a **discourse of choice** leads us to believe that acts of resistance are merely acts of vain rebellion. But this discourse ignores the ways in which meaningful social critique and defiance have moved us toward a more inclusive, just society.

The challenge educators face in connecting with students of diverse backgrounds is to develop a **critical consciousness** of the ways in which these larger discourses operate in our schools and classrooms and to care enough to question them, to challenge them, and to **advocate for our students**. Current professional teaching standards call for us to hold a much broader view of our responsibilities. To care for students who come from historically marginalized populations, we need to remember that schooling can serve either a liberating or marginalizing function. Through school, we can empower children to identify structures in society that have contributed to marginalizing their perspective and seek to maintain inequitable structures in society. We can incorporate in our lessons ways for students to identify these inequities, engage in social critique, and work for change. We can question our own practices in the face of failure and question the usefulness of our beliefs. And we can advocate for our students when they need someone to reveal, reframe, and help them cope with unfair systems.

> Consider the larger discourses affecting Lauren and Amiyah's relationship. How do the discourses of meritocracy, deficit thinking, color blindness, and choice affect Lauren's ability to connect with Amiyah?

In this chapter, we deviate slightly from the format we have developed by presenting two cases of Amiyah and DeAndre sequentially. Both cases portray the ways in which implicit discourses about race, poverty, language, and even sexuality can permeate our relationships with students and affect our abilities to not only connect with them but to empower them to engage in classroom activities and achieve at their highest potentials.

CULTURAL SYNCHRONIZATION: (MIS)INTERPRETING DISRESPECT

In 1988, Jacqueline Irvine introduced the concept of **cultural synchronization** to describe the ways in which conflict occurs in relationships between students of minority backgrounds and their majority teachers when their values, patterns of interaction, and ways of being are not aligned. Several scholars have documented the ways in which teachers and students can get out of sync with each other—where the relationship becomes characterized more by patterns of conflict and perceived disrespect than of reciprocity and understanding. For example, Wubbels, den Brok, Veldman, & van Tartwick (2006; see also Brown, 2004) found majority teachers tend to misinterpret the intentions and actions of minority students and vice versa. "[Majority] teachers may be more inclined to regard [minority] students' interpersonal messages as personally offending or threatening, and consequently the potential for conflict is higher than for conflicts with [majority] students" (p. 416).

Often, once we perceive that students are being disrespectful, we respond by trying to regain control by direct assertions of our power as adults. We threaten with consequences or bribe with rewards. The result, however, is that students feel misunderstood because they did not intend to be disrespectful. Or when resistance is meaningful, when students push back against norms and values they already reject, they feel even more controlled by a system they perceive already marginalizes them.

Because we spend so much of our time invested in relationships, we often take (mis)behavior personally without placing it in a sociohistorical or developmental context. We forget that ways of relating, style, and humor are contextual (see also Milner, 2006), and when students move from their home context into schools, meaning can get lost in translation. In their case study of a Dutch secondary teacher in a multicultural classroom, Wubbels and colleagues (Wubbels, Brekelmans, den Brok, & van Tartwijk, 2006) reported that teachers perceived multicultural classrooms to be more emotionally charged. They argued that teachers in multicultural classrooms were more likely to be confronted with their mistakes and to be persuaded to negotiate procedures, grades, and tasks. They also argued that successful teachers in diverse classrooms need to understand and clarify their own boundaries and emotions and be able to regulate their own emotions and repair relationships when faced with conflict. They need to learn how to reassess problems in a way that enables them to understand their students' behavior (Chang & Davis, 2009; Wubbels, Creton, & Holvast, 1988). We can begin the process of synchronizing with students when we model how to take ownership of our own misinterpretations. "I apologize for losing my temper. I felt like you were being disrespectful but I realize now that you did not mean any disrespect. I misjudged you and I'd like to fix what went wrong." Next, we can seek to understand students' true intentions for behavior that defies our expectations.

> In what ways were Lauren and Amiyah out of sync?
>
> How did Lauren attempt to get back in sync with Amiyah?

OBSERVING SYSTEMIC OPPRESSION

Lauren

DeAndre was a tall, kindhearted African American boy who entered our second-grade classroom in early November. He had recently moved from another state. In my experience up until that point, I'd noticed that students who enter the classroom after the beginning of the school year often go through a lengthy adjustment period. Therefore, I don't remember being worried about DeAndre until I wrote progress reports in early December. I began filling out DeAndre's report, recording his reading level as a year behind what was expected by the district in December and marking his math and writing as "below grade level." I rated him as "needing improvement" on tasks such as "cooperates easily" and "talks at appropriate times." Finally, I began filling in the comments section. I realized that none of the information I'd recorded so far adequately captured what I wanted to say about DeAndre. I wanted to tell his mom that he began each school day so happy and focused; he would enter the room and greet his peers exuberantly before settling down at his table to bend over his morning work where he would slowly etch dark, deliberate pencil lines onto his math problem set. But as the day wore on, defeat seemed to creep into him. His tall frame would begin to sag; he'd scribble angrily at his work and wear eraser marks into his papers. Most days, he grew emotionally distraught, snapping at his peers and occasionally bursting into tears. As I sat there, thinking about what to write on DeAndre's report, I decided to go down to the office to see if his cumulative folder held any information from his previous school.

I opened DeAndre's folder and was shocked to find three previous second-grade report cards from three different schools. No wonder DeAndre was frustrated and had trouble relating to his peers; he was repeating second grade for the *third* time. Immediately, I called his mom and asked her to come in for a conference. I showed his folder to my administrator and our special education coordinator, who both agreed to join the meeting. At the conference, DeAndre's mom told us that they'd moved around a lot because she was a single mom always trying to find a better job to support her family. DeAndre was retained after his first year in second grade, and she said she was worried but didn't know what to do. The next year he started second grade in a new school. DeAndre continued to struggle academically, and his mom said she begged the school to tell her why he wasn't learning. At the end of the year, he was retained again. He started his third year of second grade in another new school, and then after only one quarter, they moved to our state to live with a family member. After telling her story, she looked at us with tears in her eyes and said, "Please tell me. What is wrong with my son? Why can't he learn?"

The next day was DeAndre's last day in my classroom. He was moved into a third-grade classroom. Shortly after, he was placed in the exceptional children's program, where he received academic support from a special education teacher. He completed third grade and fourth grade at our school before moving out of our school district.

DISRUPTING SYSTEMIC OPPRESSION: MAINTAINING EXPECTATIONS, TRANSFORMING DEFICIT THINKING, AND OFFERING POSITIVE INTENT

Critical theorists like Brantlinger and Danforth (2006) argued that structures and systems in schools contribute to reproducing social and economic hierarchies in society. Earlier in Chapter 4, we highlighted the importance of revealing our underlying beliefs about relationships. Research consistently finds teachers hold differential expectations for the achievement of minority and low-income students. Moreover, minority students tend to perceive their teachers as holding lower expectations for their success. Brophy (2006) outlined the ways in which teachers communicate low expectation such as by calling on students less often, seating them farther away, seating them closer as a form of behavioral control, paying less attention and demanding less of them, offering inappropriate criticism or praise, or failing to give feedback altogether. In their comprehensive review of the literature, Murdock, Bolch, Dent, and Wilcox (2002) noted, "African-American youth may feel as though they are not likely to get a fair evaluation from their teachers" (p. 253). Moreover, when minority students perceived that their teachers held racial stereotypes or engaged in discrimination, they tended to underperform in mathematics, reported lower math self-concept and task values (Eccles, Wong, & Peck, 2006), and reported higher absences from school and a greater overall sense of alienation to school (Osborne & Walker, 2006). Lower expectations for achievement often happen when we create norms based on our White middle-class experiences and then inadvertently label anything that is different from those norms as deviant or deficit (see also Ford & Grantham, 2003). A **relationship-based approach** to interacting with students, however, presses us to interact with each child as whole, complete, and faultless (Grimmett, personal communication, 2011). A relational approach to interacting with students who hail from different backgrounds challenges us to transform our deficit thinking into dynamic thinking (Ford & Grantham, 2003).

For example, Ennis (1996) found that many teachers perceived the low-income students in their classrooms as being disinterested in the curriculum and resistant to learning. In response, they often selected pedagogies that treated students as passive participants in their own learning. But Renninger and colleagues remind us that we can transform our deficit judgments of lack of interest into dynamic thinking; their research consistently indicates that interest in academic tasks such as writing develops over time (see Figure 6.1).

Figure 6.1	Understanding How Students' *Wants* and *Needs* Vary as a Function of Their Phase of Interest

Phase of Interest	Students' Wants	Students' Needs
Phase 1: Disinterest In Phase 1, students will report they are not good at the subject (math, reading, etc.); they think learning the subject is a lot of work, and they do not revise or revisit content—mostly out of confusion about how to approach the task.	Students *want* teachers to understand how hard the new activity is for them to understand. They want teachers to help them develop strategies that will make understanding the task easier.	Students *need* teachers to offer them a limited number of concrete strategies and suggestions they can use when beginning to approach (get started) on tasks.
Phase 2: Interested in Doing It "Right" In Phase 2, students will be concerned about doing tasks the "right way"; they seek to please their teacher; they will put work into the subject but no more than they put into other assignments, and they will revise or revisit content in an effort to incorporate teachers' direct comments.	Students *want* teachers to provide them with concrete strategies for *how* to accomplish tasks.	Students *need* to be encouraged to find their *own* ways of solving problems, their *own* voice when writing, their *own* perspectives. Students need teachers to move them *away* from the belief that the teacher's way is the only "right" way.
Phase 3: Interest as Enjoyment In Phase 3, students feel connected to the subject matter and will consider themselves "good" writers, readers, or good at math. They will gladly spend time working on projects, both for school and for personal enjoyment. They revise a great deal, mostly to "make it sound right" to themselves. They appreciate recognition of their work and dislike feedback when it feels like the commentator is trying to tell them how to write.	Students *want* freedom to be autonomous—to express their own voice, to solve problems their own way, and to have their perspective validated.	Students *need* teachers who can "temper their enthusiasm for their way of doing things" (p. 82) with a broader understanding of the multiple perspectives, audiences, power structures, and shared understandings in the field.

(Continued)

Figure 6.1 (Continued)

Phase of Interest	Students' Wants	Students' Needs
Phase 4: Interested in Excellence		
In Phase 4, students have an awareness of their place in the greater field. They gladly spend time working on projects, both for school and for personal enjoyment. They gladly revisit or revise to not only improve the product, but also their skills. They welcome all constructive feedback and will get frustrated when only praise is offered with no suggestions for improvement.	Students *want* to find a balance between their need to be autonomous, to have a voice, and their personal standards *and* to meet more widely accepted standards, convince an audience.	Students *need* their teachers to continue to be challenged, to practice and improve their skills and widen their repertoire of strategies, and to continue to receive and interpret constructive feedback on their work.

Source: Adapted from Lipstein & Renninger (2007).

In their study of the development of interest in writing, Lipstein and Renninger (2007) found students' interest in writing developed as a function of their wants and needs surrounding writing being met. When we deconstruct a lack of interest in terms of students' wants and needs, we can begin to think dynamically about how we can develop interests for academic content by meeting students' wants and needs (Ford & Grantham, 2003).

When we think more dynamically about the deficits we perceive in our students, we offer them what researcher Becky Bailey (2000) called **positive intent**: "Positive intent has the power to turn children around, changing aggressive children into cooperative members of your classroom and helping bullies learn other ways of feeling in control and safe" (p. 159). Offering positive intent involves monitoring when we have deficit thoughts and remembering that it is impossible to accurately assess the intentions of others. Offering positive intent involves making judgments about misbehavior or disrespect that reminds us that students are constantly trying to meet their needs. When we offer positive intent to students, we can create teaching moments helping students develop the skills they need to effectively and appropriately meet their needs. Blackburn (2005) described how transforming our thinking from deficit to dynamic can position students in a place of power where they feel competent and autonomous.

> In what ways did Lauren fall into
> the traps of deficit thinking?
>
> In what ways did Lauren resist
> the traps of deficit thinking?
>
> How was Lauren able to transform
> her thinking from deficit to dynamic?

It is not merely the enactment of our unintentional prejudices that leads to the relationship and achievement gaps but, rather, (a) the systematic underfunding and segregation of schools across the nation; (b) the differential use of tracking, retention, and placement in special education and gifted programs; and (c) the higher rates of teacher turnover and attrition that disproportionately affect minorities and the poor (Brantlinger & Danforth, 2006; Gay, 2006; Milner, 2006). These structures are vestiges of discrimination that we often routinely accept because they align with the discourses of meritocracy and choice. When we become conscious, however, to systemic oppression that happens in schools, we can become critical of the ways in which we have institutionalized racism and classism in schools. For the past 30 years, racial and gender disparities have abounded in school disciplinary actions and suspensions, with African American males experiencing the harshest practices. Minority students tend to be referred for less serious infractions more frequently. Low-income students tend to receive more severe punishments that are often delivered in unprofessional and public ways (Gay, 2006).

European Americans often have a hard time confronting our history of discrimination in this country (Lawrence & Tatum, 1997; Tatum, 1997). We can encounter feelings of shame and guilt when we become conscious of the legacy of privilege and power. We often want to retreat into the discourse of color blindness, denying the unwitting role we can play in perpetuating injustice, as a way to protect ourselves. But Tatum (1997) reminded us that there have always been *White allies*, advocates for those who are marginalized by society who resisted participating in oppressive structures. To be race, class, and gender conscious does not mean that we believe that there are inherent differences between groups. Rather, consciousness involves recognizing that society treats groups differently and can lead to dismantling injustice. Anderson (2007) noted that even the framers of the 14th Amendment to the U.S. Constitution were race conscious—struggling with issues of how to extend and protect the rights of members of different racial and ethnic groups.

> In what ways was DeAndre subject to structures in the school that often lead to the underachievement of diverse students?
>
> How did Lauren disrupt the cycle?

WHAT DOES IT MEAN TO BE CULTURALLY COMPETENT IN OUR RELATIONSHIPS?

When reviewing the literature on culturally responsive management and instruction, four factors emerge as central (Brown, 2003; Gay, 2006; Milner, 2006):

1. Effective teachers model respect for diverse students during instructional, social and personal interactions.

2. Effective teachers respond explicitly to the needs of diverse students.

3. Effective teachers are assertive about appropriate social and academic behavioral expectations. They do not assume that students know how to be successful in school, and they view conflict with students as a reflection of not knowing, understanding, or accepting school norms.

4. Effective teachers develop a responsive, integrative, and problem-based curriculum that empowers students to become involved in their schools and their communities (Ladson-Billings, 2001).

In 1997, Shade, Kelly and Oberg developed a framework for understanding the factors that lead to establishing a culturally compatible classroom. Drawing from their work and the work we reviewed for this chapter, we provide some guidelines for developing cultural competence when interacting with students of diverse backgrounds (see Figure 6.2). Developing relationships with students of diverse backgrounds requires learning something about the sociohistorical context (Beaty-O'Ferrall, Green, & Hanna, 2010). As students seek to understand their own identities, the meaning they associate with historical events that have affected their group and how they position us as teachers and representatives of school can dramatically affect our relationships.

Figure 6.2 Factors Contributing to Culturally Competent Classroom Relationships

In-Depth Knowledge of the Socio-Historical Context of Student's Culture

Personal Determination to Establish a Strong Teacher-Student Relationship with Each Student

Identify and Develop Strategies to Build Bridges Between Student's Home Culture and School Culture

Reveal Implicit Knowledge, Skills, and Systems that Contribute to Student's Exclusion

Develop Extensive Variety of Instructional Strategies to Develop Competence

Set Aside Time to Systematically Reflect on Relationship Quality

Culturally Competent Classroom Relationships

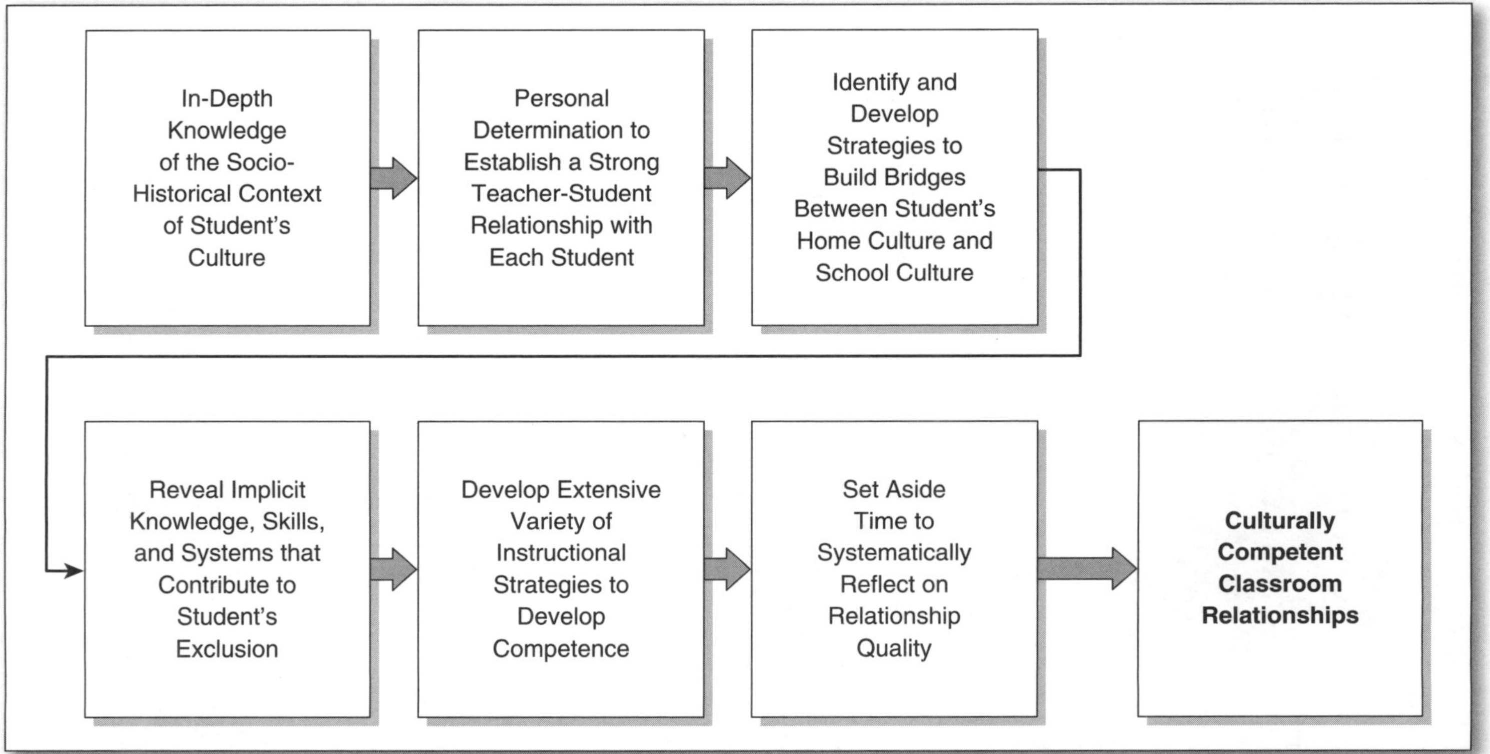

Source: Adapted from Shade, Kelly, & Oberg (1997, p. 138).

Learning to interact with someone who has different life experiences and ways of viewing the world can be difficult. It requires us to make a commitment; allocate energy, intellectual, and emotional resources; and make a personal commitment to developing individual relationships with each student in our classrooms. When faced with conflict or resistance from students, we can frame conflict as opportunities to (a) learn new strategies to understand and connect with students, (b) learn ways to involve students in understanding and solving the challenges we face in society, and (c) learn new ways to support students' mastery of the content we teach.

> With Amiyah and DeAndre, Lauren demonstrated a personal determination to develop a relationship and support their learning despite feeling disappointed and overwhelmed.
>
> In the past, what obstacles have you experienced that kept you from committing to developing relationships with some populations of students?

Unfortunately, knowledge of students' culture and a commitment to develop relationships is often not enough. The literature on teacher education and teacher professional development is fraught with case studies of teachers reporting feeling frustrated by their interactions with students and their inabilities to connect. This reflects, in part, a failure of teacher education programs to devote time to tackling the tough questions and be able to systematically place new teachers in diverse classrooms. But this may also reflect the great diversity that lies *within* each culture and each individual. Research consistently suggests that effective teachers of diverse students are creative. They use what they know about their curricular standards and about their students to identify new ways to help students connect with the content and new ways to build bridges between students' home and school cultures (Ladson-Billings, 2001). Effective teachers of diverse students know that the curriculum needs to be personally meaningful to their student population. And what is meaningful to one population may not be relevant to another. There is a phrase in scrapbooking called *lifting*. It refers to viewing another artists' page and using it as a heuristic to guide your composition. The content of the pages will be different—but the structural elements will appear similar. To be effective with diverse students we must become authorities in pedagogy—learning how to see potential in other teachers' management and instructional methods and learning how to "lift" and modify methods.

Understanding context, making a commitment, and finding a way to connect with diverse students is merely the first step in developing a culturally competent classroom. Culturally competent classrooms are characterized by a critical consciousness toward the curriculum, school, and community. Culturally competent teachers aren't afraid to involve their students in asking the tough questions about education: Why is this content important? How will we use it? How does it make our life and our community better?

Beverly Tatum (1997) also discussed the importance of teaching children how to spot oppressive discourses and practices in society (p. 46). She describes coming to a realization that a text she loved as a child, *The Boxcar Children*, contained chauvinistic representations of girls.

> After reading several pages of this together, I decided to say something to my then seven-year-old son. I asked if he knew what sexism was. He did not, so I explained that it was when girls were treated differently than boys just because they were girls, and I pointed out some of the examples and discussed the unfairness of it. (p. 47)

Tatum goes on to argue that learning to spot sexist, racist, classist, homophobic, and intolerant discourses in our curricula and media is an important skill for *all* children to develop. "We are better able to resist the negative impact of oppressive messages when we see them coming than when they are invisible to us" (p. 47). Learning to identify deficit messages represents one of many critical competencies diverse students need in order to participate fully in society.

> Take a moment to critically evaluate your curriculum.
>
> What additional competencies do the diverse students in your class need to acquire in order to fully participate in their community?

Finally, as Lauren reflected on Amiyah, we sometimes need to acknowledge we don't have it all figured out. Consistently, the literature documents the important role that systematic, thoughtful reflection plays in promoting critical consciousness. In their study of professional development designed to promote critical consciousness, Lawrence and Tatum (1997) found that many teachers were uncomfortable thinking about and discussing issues of oppression: "I am thirty-five years old and I never really started thinking about race too much until now, and that makes me feel uncomfortable. . . . No one taught us. That's what I tell my students" (p. 163).

As teacher educators in southern states, we find that our students often express the opposing view. They feel inundated with discussions of race and class. Cultural competence, however, begins with a commitment to systematically and routinely reflect on the status of instruction, management, and relationships with diverse students. According to Lawrence and Tatum (1997), this can include reflecting on the extent to which (a) your expectations are consistent across all students for motivation and performance; (b) you seek out the perspective of colleagues of color; (c) you challenge oppressive behaviors or structures in the school and among staff; (d) you advocate for children of color (with other teachers and administrators); (e) you question the need for special education assessments, grouping, or testing practices for diverse students; and (f) you actively assist children in spotting and challenging stereotypes. Lawrence and Tatum (1997) argued that the teachers in their professional development courses committed to making emancipation the business of their teaching adopted strategies that "empowered all students, not just the few" (p. 175).

CONNECT TO YOUR PRACTICE

Analyze Your Unconscious Behaviors

Category	Student	Why?	Identify Underlying Discourses
If you could keep one student for another year, whom would you pick?			
If you could devote all of your attention to a student who concerns you a great deal, whom would you pick?			
If a parent were to drop in unannounced for a conference, whose child would you be the least prepared to talk about?			
If your class were to be reduced by one child, whom would you feel relieved to have removed?			

Consider your classroom and reflect on the different types of relationships you build with students. Select for each of the following categories a student that demonstrates (a) your attachment, (b) your concern, (c) your feelings of disconnection, and (d) your feelings of alienation. We know this can be difficult because no teacher wants to believe he or she ignores or is unfair to students, but it is important to reveal how underlying discourses of meritocracy, deficit thinking, color blindness, and choice can affect our ability to build relationships.

Source: Adapted from Shade, Kelly, & Oberg (1997, p. 48).

KEY TERMS

Advocate for our students: Empowering students to work against discourses that marginalize them or create inequities in society.

Critical consciousness: An awareness of the ways in which discourses of meritocracy, deficit thinking, color blindness, and choice affect our schools, classrooms, and communities, and therefore, our students.

Cultural synchronization: Alignment of individuals' values, interaction styles, and ways of being; lack of alignment can lead to conflict.

Discourse of choice: A way of thinking that holds that resisting cultural norms is ineffective and self-centered.

Discourse of color blindness: A way of thinking that holds that it is better for society to ignore qualities such as race, ethnicity, religion, and sexual orientation than acknowledge those differences.

Discourse of deficit thinking: A way of thinking that holds that those who do not fit the stereotype of the "American Ideal" will be unsuccessful in life unless they are fixed.

Discourse of meritocracy: A way of thinking that holds that individuals receive what they deserve—for example, that hard work leads to a well-paying job.

Positive intent: When a teacher recognizes how prevalent discourses and deficit thinking cause them to perceive students' actions as misbehavior or disrespect and instead, the teacher recognizes all students' actions as ways students seek to meet their own needs.

Relationship-based management approaches: Classroom management practice in which the teacher encourages each student to take shared ownership of the classroom environment and their behavior and in which behavioral expectations are adjusted to meet the needs of each student.

Teacher expectations: Teachers who hold high expectations for students recognize that as teachers, they are responsible for creating optimal learning environments in which all students can achieve their maximum potential.

RESOURCES FOR TEACHERS

Blackburn, M. (2005). Talking together for a change: Examining positioning between teachers and queer youth. In J. A. Vadeboncoeur & L. Patel (Eds.), *Re/constructing "the adolescent": Sign, symbol, and body* (pp. 249–270). New York, NY: Peter Lang.

Brown, D. F. (2003). Urban teachers' use of culturally responsive management strategies. *Theory Into Practice, 42*, 277–282.

Curran, M. E. (2003). Linguistic diversity and classroom management. *Theory Into Practice, 42*, 334–340.

Davis, H. A., Gableman, M., & Wingfield, R. (2011). "She let us be smart": Low-income African American first-grade students' understandings of teacher closeness and influence. *Journal of Classroom Interaction: The Structure and Function of Teacher Management and Care in Classroom Settings, 46*[Special issue], 4–16.

DeAngelis, T. (2009, February). Micro-Aggressions. *American Psychological Association's Monitor on Psychology*, 43–46.

Eccles, J. S., Wong, C. A., & Peck, S. C. (2006). Ethnicity as a social context for the development of African-American adolescents. *Journal of School Psychology, 44*, 407–426.

Ford, D. Y., & Grantham, T. C. (2003). Providing access for culturally diverse gifted students: From deficit to dynamic thinking. *Theory Into Practice, 42*, 217–225.

Howard, T. C. (2003). Culturally relevant pedagogy: Ingredients for critical teacher reflection. *Theory Into Practice, 42*, 195–202.

Ladson-Billings, G. (2001). *Crossing over to Canaan: The journey of new teachers in diverse classrooms* (pp. 101–122). San Francisco, CA: Jossey-Bass.

Lareau, A. (1987). Social class differences in family-school relationships: The importance of cultural capital. *Sociology of Education, 60*, 73–85.

Lawrence, S., & Tatum, B. D. (1997). Teachers in transition: The impact of antiracist professional development on classroom practice. *Teachers College Record, 99*, 162–178.

Lipstein, R. L., & Renninger, K. A. (2007, March). Interest for writing: How teachers can make a difference. *English Journal, 96*, 79–85.

Milner, H. R. (2003). Teacher reflection and race in cultural contexts: History, meaning, and methods in teaching. *Theory Into Practice, 42*, 173–180.

Shade, B. J., Kelly, C., & Oberg, M. (1997). *Creating culturally responsive classrooms: Psychology in the Classroom.* Washington, DC: American Psychological Association.

Tatum, B. (1997). *"Why are all the black kids sitting together in the cafeteria?" and other conversations about race.* New York. NY: Basic Books.

Weiner, L. (2004). Why is classroom management so vexing to urban teachers? *Theory Into Practice, 42*, 305–312.

PART III

Management as a Function of Teacher Self-Regulation

7

What Does It Mean to Self-Regulate My Classroom Management Tasks?

OBSERVING TEACHER SELF-REGULATION

Lauren

I was first introduced to the world of ADHD when I was student teaching in a first grade classroom. Three of our students were diagnosed with ADHD and were a challenge to the existing management system in our classroom, but one student's difficulties far surpassed the others. When Alex's behavior was good, he was a joy to be around. He smiled easily, gave big bear hugs, answered questions insightfully, and came up with creative solutions to problems. But on a bad day, Alex would quite literally enter the classroom swinging. With a scowl plastered on his face, he verbally and physically lashed out at others, defied classroom rules and procedures, and refused to complete assignments. Alex's behavior was out of control more often than it was under control, which made the classroom an exhausting, frustrating place for him, his teachers, and his peers. We quickly decided that because Alex's behavior was so overwhelming, we needed to focus on very concrete behavioral goals in order to help him better integrate into the classroom.

During whole-group lessons, Alex was distracted and was a distraction to others. The students sat cross-legged on a carpet in the front of the room, but Alex never stayed in one place for long. He would slowly inch his way to the edge of the carpet, where he would hang on the table legs, crawl under chairs, and fling his legs and arms around. Such disassociation from the group was synonymous with disassociation from the lesson; Alex rarely participated, and when he did, he called out answers with abandon rather than following hand-raising procedures. I decided to experiment with seating to find out if there was a better arrangement for Alex. I chose three spots in the classroom I thought might serve as alternate seating places for Alex during a group lesson: (a) a reading area that was adjacent to the carpet, (b) his desk, and (c) a special chair with the class mascot on it. Each day Alex sat in one of these different places, and I took notes about his behavior and participation. After two weeks of trying each seating arrangement multiple times, I came to the conclusion that none of the areas worked. When he sat in the reading area, Alex's participation declined even further. He threw tantrums when he sat at his desk. And while he was happy in the mascot chair, he spoke out constantly when he was seated there. Frustrated that none of the options were working, I pulled Alex aside and asked him to tell me what he thought of his special seats. I was blown away by his insightful answers. Alex said that the reading area was nice because no one else was bothering him but that he couldn't see me very well. He told me that he hated sitting at his desk because he thought it meant he was being bad. I realized that we'd used it as a consequence in the past and that it was logical he'd associate it with negative emotions. And he revealed that he thought the mascot chair was a reward, which explained why he ignored the classroom rules when he was there.

I mulled over Alex's responses that night and hit on a new idea. The next day I told Alex I had a special place for him on the carpet. After a few tries, we found a spot that was slightly removed from the rest of the group but that was right up front and close to the teacher. When he sat in this spot, Alex was able to focus for longer periods of time; he raised his hand more often, called out less often, and contributed on-topic ideas to group discussions. He told me that he liked it because none of the other kids could bother him and that he liked being with the teacher. I noted that he made eye contact with me more often, particularly when he was waiting to be called on, and that he often focused on the visual stimuli related to the lesson. It took about three weeks to find the right seating arrangement for Alex, but it made a big impact on his ability to positively engage in whole-group lessons.

THINKING SYSTEMATICALLY ABOUT CLASSROOM MANAGEMENT

When something goes wrong with our management design, our instinct is to look for a quick fix—a magic bullet that will solve the problem. Students, however, are more complex. Some students, like Alex, require that we develop individualized plans to help them succeed in the classroom and develop the skills that allow them to be in command of their emotions and behavior. In this chapter, we address the dilemma of understanding and designing effective management plans for students who struggle to control their behavior and emotions. We approach management problems from a problem-solving, self-regulated learning perspective (Franke, Carpenter, Fennema, Ansell, & Behrend, 1998; Franke, Carpenter, Levi, & Fennema, 2001; Zimmerman, 2004). The self-regulated learning framework involves a three-stage process to help teachers problem solve in ways that promote and sustain changes in themselves and their students.

In this chapter, we use a self-regulated learning framework to highlight Lauren's attempts to connect with and support Alex, a student diagnosed with Attention Deficit Hyperactivity Disorder (ADHD). Why did we choose to focus on Lauren's relationship with a student with ADHD? In 2002, Greene and colleagues reported that teachers experienced heightened stress working with students with ADHD (Greene, Beszterczey, Katzenstein, Park, & Goring, 2002). Teachers perceived that students with ADHD disrupted the learning process and required more support than students without ADHD. They also reported experiencing more frustration and feeling less satisfied with teaching. We selected ADHD as an example of one type of student who struggles to control his or her classroom behavior. However, Marzano, Marzano, and Pickering (2003) noted that a significant population of children in our country struggle with a variety of physical, environmental, and psychological stressors, including homelessness, depression and suicide, poverty, alcoholism and drug addiction, and abuse that manifest in difficulties regulating behavior and emotion.

Why Are Students With ADHD So Challenging?

ADHD is a neurobiological condition that affects a child's ability to monitor his or her thoughts and behavior and inhibit his or her impulses. Students with ADHD often exhibit excessive motor activity (i.e., need to be in motion). Moreover, 50% of the children diagnosed with ADHD also qualify for special education services, suggesting ADHD occurs concurrently with other learning and behavioral disabilities (Arcia, Frank, Sánchez-LaCay, & Fernáindez, 2000).

In the classroom, difficulties to exert self-control manifest in challenges such as starting and staying on task, following directions, making transitions, interacting with others, and producing consistent work (for manifestations of ADHD, including manifestations of side effects of medication, see Pierangelo & Guiliani, 2003, pp. 6–7, and Arcia et al., 2000, pp. 94–95). Teachers of students with ADHD report that these students require a high degree of intervention and close monitoring over short intervals of time (Arcia et al., 2000). These interventions are often complex and may change over the academic year. "You will need to revamp, revise, and modify your behavior management systems frequently" (Reif, 1993, p. 13).

Moreover, successful interventions require teachers to devote a great deal of time to qualifying and quantifying the problem and target behaviors. Successful interventions also may require teachers to think holistically about the nature of the problem. Often, students with ADHD struggle to form meaningful peer relationships (Soodak & McCarthy, 2006). Impulse control can affect the abilities of students with ADHD to work with peers in collaborative groups, to navigate typical peer conflicts, to develop and share deeper understandings of themselves and others, and to sustain relationships across the usual school transitions (Saunders & Chambers, 1996; Shapiro, 2010; Zentell, Craig, & Kuster, 2011; see Chapter 5).

Unfortunately, the behavior of students with ADHD is often "misperceived as purposeful non-compliance" (Pierangelo & Guiliani, 2003, p. 52). Indeed Arcia and colleagues (2000) found the teachers in their study were more likely to attribute classroom misbehavior of students with ADHD to deficits in the children's environment. "According to the teachers the children would benefit from: a stable home environment; more reading less television; a male role-model; family counseling; more discipline at home; extra attention; and active parental involvement in teaching and homework" (Arcia et al., 2000, p. 96). They argued that because teachers attributed the source of the problem to factors outside of their control, it hindered their attempts to provide effective interventions and to develop a plan to bring about desired social and learning behaviors. Interestingly, in observations of teachers interacting with students with and without ADHD, observers recorded teachers had increased rates of both positive and negative interactions with students with ADHD. In other words, it is not necessarily that teachers have poorer quality interactions overall, simply that they appear to devote significantly more time to interacting with students with ADHD (Greene et al., 2002).

Self-Sustaining Generative Change

In their studies of teacher problem solving, Franke and colleagues (Franke et al., 1998; Franke et al., 2001) identified a subset of teachers who had developed strategies that allowed for them to engage in **self-sustaining generative change.** "Generativity refers to individuals' abilities to continue to add to their understanding. When individuals learn with understanding, they can apply their knowledge to learn new topics and solve new and unfamiliar problems" (Franke et al., 2001, pp. 655–656). Thus, teachers who were capable of self-sustaining generative change were able to frame classroom problems in a way that promoted a deeper understanding of their students and their own teaching.

> The kind of change we envision involves teachers changing in ways that provide a basis for continued growth and problem solving—what we call self-sustaining, generative change. Self-sustaining, generative change does not involve acquiring a set of procedures to implement with fidelity; rather it frequently entails teachers making changes in their basic epistemological perspectives, their knowledge of what it means to learn, as well as their conceptions of classroom practice. (Franke et al., 1998, p. 67)

The process begins when we view ourselves as capable of creating and elaborating on our own professional knowledge—when we view ourselves as problem solvers. Virginia Richardson (1994) first identified teachers who engaged in **practical inquiry**—that is, teachers who observed and thought deeply and systematically about their own classrooms. Indeed, teachers who generate knowledge that transforms their practice tend to focus on understanding student thinking, listen to and carefully observe students' thinking, and are not afraid to rethink their beliefs and classroom practices. When faced with an instructional problem, they articulate problem types and the strategies used by students that are successful and unsuccessful. They strive to make connections among different types of problems and strategies in ways that reveal underlying beliefs, principles, insights, and skills that lead to a deeper understanding of their own and students' thinking.

UNDERSTANDING THE PHASES OF
TEACHER SELF-REGULATION

Systematic, flexible, creative problem solving is one of the most cognitively complex skills we develop throughout our lifetime. Often the skills that enable educators to be effective problem solvers are learned implicitly by observing and emulating the behaviors of our parents, teachers, and mentors. To our knowledge, few teacher preparation programs provide opportunities for preservice teachers to engage in problem-solving behaviors. In the following sections, we describe Zimmerman's (2004) three-phase model of **self-regulation** (see Figure 7.1). Again, *self-regulated learning frameworks employ a three-stage process approach to helping teachers problem solve in ways that promote and sustain changes in themselves and their students.* We describe different components of each phase and apply each phase to understand how engaging in specific behaviors can lead to both reducing behavior problems and self-sustaining generative change.

Forethought/Planning Phase

During the **forethought/planning phase,** the goal is to frame a classroom management problem as a task, to evaluate each dimension of the task, and to evaluate your resources to accomplish the task. Earlier we noted the research suggests that when it comes to interacting with children who have ADHD, we may first need to learn more about the disorder and how it can manifest in different types of disruptive behaviors in the classroom. A better understanding of the disorder can help us set more reasonable goals and plan our lessons more strategically. During this phase, we also need to evaluate our personal resources: Do you feel confident you have the strategies and resources you need to meet the student's needs? Are you interested in understanding the child's thinking and in finding a creative solution that works for both of you? Are you oriented toward developing a deeper understanding of

| Figure 7.1 | Zimmerman's (2004) Phases and Subcomponents of Self-Regulated Learning |

Performance Phase

Self-Control

Imagery
Self-instruction
Attention focusing
Task strategies

Self-Observation

Self-recording
Self-experimentation

Forethought Phase

Task Analysis

Goal setting
Strategic planning

Self-Motivation Beliefs

Self-efficacy
Outcome expectations
Intrinsic interest/value
Learning goal orientation

Self-Reflection Phase

Self-Judgment

Self-evaluation
Casual attribution

Self-Reaction

Self-satisfaction/affect
Adaptive/defensive

Source: Zimmerman (2004)

the factors that lead to ADHD students' success in your classroom?

In Table 7.1 of Connect to Practice, provided at the end of this chapter, we further break down ways to be more systematic and thoughtful about the behavior that is disrupting your class. As part of their practical inquiry, teachers who were engaged in self-sustaining generative change appeared to collect data from their students concerning their thinking and strategies and use this data to set goals and identify interventions. It is critical when setting out to collect data on problem behaviors that we push ourselves to collect data at the most granular level. For example, it was not enough for Lauren to record the frequency of how often Alex called out in class. She learned that developing a deep understanding of the source of Alex's impulse control required her to collect data on what he was calling out, whether he was demonstrating some impulse control by using an inside voice and raising his hand, and how his impulse control changed as a function of where he was and who he was with in the classroom.

Applied Behavior Analysis

It is important to understand that underlying successful interventions for students with ADHD or other severe behavior problems are the objective observation of the behavior. Often this is challenging and may require you to video yourself or ask a colleague to observe and give feedback. Many districts throughout the country employ Functional Behavioral Assessment (FBA) Checklists (see http://www.apa.org/ed/schools/cpse/activities/class-management.aspx) to evaluate the antecedents and consequences of disruptive behavior in the classroom. Especially when we are feeling overwhelmed, these checklists, by focusing our attention on specific aspects of the student's behavior, can provide invaluable information and can help us get some emotional distance and objectivity. Whether you develop your own tools or use an FBA, it is important to record the frequency of the problem behavior and the outcomes it produces.

Selecting Interventions

Once we have gathered enough information to feel confident that we have analyzed the task and understand the source of the problem, we need to identify an intervention that addresses the problem. Remember, Lauren's first attempts at designing an intervention for Alex were unsuccessful. She notes how important it was to talk with Alex and try to understand his thinking about sitting with the group. Students often know a lot more about their behavior than we give them credit for. In the Connect to Practice, a teacher resource at the end of the chapter, we provide an overview of interventions described in the ADHD literature (see Tables 7.4–7.7). We organize them into four categories: (a) **interpersonal interventions**, (b) **instructional interventions**, (c) **environmental interventions**, and (d) **behavioral interventions**. The purpose of interpersonal interventions is to increase the ADHD student's relational engagement including an awareness and monitoring of his or her behavior on other members of the class. The purpose of instructional interventions is to increase engagement in the task by modifying how instruction is delivered to better meet the needs of a child with ADHD. The purpose of environmental interventions is to increase structure in the environment to meet the ADHD student's needs for clarity and predictability. The purpose of behavioral interventions is to increase the frequency of appropriate behavior while decreasing the frequency of inappropriate behavior through the use of reinforcers or punishments. Several authors provide interventions specific to mathematics and literacy activities (see Pierangelo & Guiliani, 2003, pp. 64–96; Reif, 1993, pp. 59–92). Additionally, Reif (1993, pp. 73–83) outlined the principles that underlie behavioral interventions.

It can be critically important when selecting an intervention to implement in your classroom to involve parents, previous teachers, and school support staff. We designed Tables 7.1 through 7.3 of Connect to Practice at the end of the chapter to include a column for a team of teachers to work together to identify successful and unsuccessful strategies attempted in the past. When working with a family, you may want to make copies of these charts to share with parents and collect information on what strategies have been tried and found successful at home. ADHD students tend to achieve the most success with clear consistent expectations. Successful interventions for students with different characteristics, needs, or abilities may involve clarifying for students when the demands of the classroom and expectations for behavior across home and school differ.

Consider Lauren's approach to Alex's behavior.
Where do you see evidence of planning behaviors?

Performance/Monitoring Phase

During the **performance/monitoring phase,** the goal is to focus on implementing the intervention you selected and collect data on its results. Earlier, we noted that teachers of students with ADHD report that these students require a high degree of intervention and close monitoring over short intervals of time (Arcia et al., 2000). During the performance phase, the goal is to set a period of time for evaluating the strategy and focus your attention on implementing the intervention consistently. This can be challenging. We often want to shift back into old ways of interacting because they feel familiar and are easier than changing. It is important during this time period to collect data on your implementation. Consider keeping a reflective journal or developing a spreadsheet to record your observations and experiences during the intervention (see Table 7.2 in Connect to Practice for a step-by-step process).

Consider Lauren's approach to Alex's behavior.
Where do you see evidence of
monitoring both her teaching behaviors
and their effects on Alex's behavior?

Self-Reflection/Evaluation Phase

During the **self-reflection/evaluation phase,** the goal is to step back from all the data you have collected during the planning phase and the monitoring phase and evaluate the ways in which the intervention you implemented succeeded in bringing about the outcomes you identified (see Table 7.3 in Connect to Practice). During this phase, the challenge is to make attributions of success and failure that are adaptive and that lead us toward continued classroom problem solving. Adaptive attributions include those that focus our attention on the factors that lie within our control. How might behavior problems be a function of the classroom environment, the classroom relationships, or the students' attempts to gratify his or her unmet needs?

Productive Reflection

One of the challenges we face in reflecting on our teaching can be focusing our attention on the factors we can influence. Teaching is an incredibly emotional practice, and in the face of both successes and failures, we can lose our attention to details or shift our focus away from factors that lie within our control. As we mentioned earlier, research suggests that teachers are more likely to attribute classroom misbehavior of students with ADHD to perceived deficits in the children's home environment. Elizabeth Davis (2006) however, studied the characteristics of novice teachers who were **productive** in their reflection; that is, they tended to record information and evaluate events in a way that led them toward increasingly more effective planning. Teachers who were productive in their reflection tended to evidence four characteristics:

1. They were specific, accurate, and objective in their reporting of classroom events.

2. They sought to integrate information from across a variety of sources.

3. They maintained their focus on the child's perspective and factors they could control in themselves and their classrooms.

4. They sought to identify a plan of action for the future that directly drew from their insights.

Productive reflection can be challenging. It requires us to devote time to honestly reflect on classroom events—time we often perceive we do not have. It can be challenging to set aside the time because our experiences of disappointment and frustration lead us to blame factors we cannot control, and our experiences of fatigue leave us feeling discouraged. But consistently, research suggests the insights gained from the process of productive reflection—because we are engaged in generating new knowledge of ourselves and classroom problems—can leave us feeling empowered to face challenges in our classroom.

> Consider Lauren's approach to Alex's behavior.
> What role did Alex's feedback play in promoting
> productive reflection on the intervention?

SHIFTING THE LOCUS OF RESPONSIBILITY FOR MANAGING BEHAVIOR

It is important to remember that the long-term goal of any classroom intervention is ultimately to help students develop the ability to regulate their own behavior in the classroom. In this chapter, we dealt with the challenges teachers face to interact with students who struggle with impulse control. Like some other students in the classroom, students with ADHD need additional support to develop strategies to respond appropriately to their impulses and maintain their focus on learning. As students transition to adulthood, however, they need to learn to regulate their behavior independently. We can lay a foundation for student self-regulation of behavior by involving students in planning interventions, monitoring their own behavior, and reflecting on what strategies are working or not working. As students become more aware of triggers in the classroom and develop the ability to reflect on their own behavior, they can begin to assume more responsibility for self-regulation. Finally, involving students in this process not only helps students to understand their responsibilities, but it can also improve our relationship with them. Remember in Chapter 1, students' behavior is often driven by their needs to feel connected, competent, and autonomous in the classroom.

Consider Lauren's approach to Alex's behavior. How did Lauren's intervention *improve* her understanding of and relationship with Alex?

CONNECT TO YOUR PRACTICE

Using Self-Regulatory Skills to Improve Relationship Quality: Systematic Tools for Planning, Monitoring, Reflecting

Table 7.1 Document Systematic Planning

Planning			Documenting My Problem Solving
The purpose of planning activities is to develop a clearer understanding of the student's beliefs, perceptions, and needs; clarify your instructional and management goals; and select an appropriate intervention.			
Step 1	Understand the source of the behavior problem	What do you need to know about your students' background?	
	Behavioral manifestations in the classroom	How will I record the frequency of behaviors, changes across classroom settings, antecedents and consequences etc.? Do I need to make a chart?	
Step 2	Identify desired behavior	Try to set objectives based on the frequencies observed in Step 1.	
	Set reasonable goals	It is important to set attainable goals. Consider the extent to which the objectives you set are reasonable.	

(Continued)

Table 7.1 (Continued)

Planning			Documenting My Problem Solving
	The purpose of planning activities is to develop a clearer understanding of the student's beliefs, perceptions, and needs; clarify your instructional and management goals; and select an appropriate intervention.		
Step 3	Identify an intervention (See Tables 7.4 through 7.7 for potential ADHD interventions)	What interventions seem to address the source of the problem? Given your personal and professional resources, what interventions are sustainable?	
	Understand the principles that underlie effective implementation	What information/resources do you need to successfully implement the intervention?	
	Elicit student feedback	How can you frame this intervention in a way that the student is invested in participating?	

Table 7.2 Monitor Fidelity to an Intervention

Monitoring		*The purpose of monitoring activities is to (1) collect data on your fidelity to implementing the intervention over a sufficient period of time and (2) collect data on changes in the child's perceptions and behavior.*	Documenting My Problem Solving
Step 4	Set reasonable evaluation period	Consider implementing during natural shifts in the curriculum (i.e., introduction of a new unit). Consider how long it may take to see improvements.	
	Monitor your implementation of the intervention	Consider your commitment and willingness to adhere to the principles in Step 3.	
Step 5	Provide feedback to students (see concept of "noticing")	Consider strategies to be more systematic and frequent in providing feedback during the intervention.	

(Continued)

Table 7.2 (Continued)

Monitoring		*The purpose of monitoring activities is to (1) collect data on your fidelity to implementing the intervention over a sufficient period of time and (2) collect data on changes in the child's perceptions and behavior.*	Documenting My Problem Solving
Step 6	Collect data	Consider designing a spreadsheet or keeping a reflective journal to record your behavior during the intervention.	
	Implementation	Did you modify the intervention along the way?	
	Outcomes	What happened? Try to record at the most granular level.	
	Student feedback	Consider the students' perspectives. How do they feel about the intervention? Do they perceive it to be supporting their learning?	
	Child focus	How might the child's behavior reflect his or her attempts to meet his or her need to feel competent, autonomous, or connected?	
	Future oriented	Given what you learned, can you identify 1 or 2 tangible strategies you can implement?	

Table 7.3 Evaluate the Effectiveness of an Intervention

Reflecting		Documenting My Problem Solving
	The purpose of reflection activities is to synthesize across your planning and monitoring data to evaluate the effectiveness of the intervention and then make a plan of action for the future.	
Step 7	Integration	Look across the data you collected. What patterns do you see? How do you make sense of discrepant behaviors?

Table 7.4 Interpersonal Interventions for Students With ADHD

Interpersonal Interventions	The purpose of interpersonal interventions is to increase the ADHD child's relational engagement including an awareness and monitoring of his or her behavior on other members of the class.	Strategies That I'd Like to Try/ Strategies That Work for Me
Procedures for gaining student's attention	This might include private signals and/or discrete cues for behaviors.	
Increase immediacy behaviors	This might include increasing your physical proximity, and eye contact, and introducing appropriate forms of touch such as placing a hand on the student's shoulder.	
Voice control	See Reif (1993, p. 170)	
Provide response cards	This might include making the student some Yes/No or A,B,C,D, response cards or providing a small white board for him or her to write down an immediate response.	
System for frequent feedback	This might involve using a timer on a watch or phone to prompt you to check in with the student more frequently.	

Interpersonal Interventions	The purpose of interpersonal interventions is to increase the ADHD child's relational engagement including an awareness and monitoring of his or her behavior on other members of the class.	Strategies That I'd Like to Try/ Strategies That Work for Me
Avoid mixed messages	This involves delaying your own impulse to provide corrective feedback and praise at the same time. Might include carrying a notepad to record praise and/or corrective feedback to give at a later time.	
Gentle discipline	This involves using small corrections and natural consequences (Reeve, 2006). It might require integrating a system for frequent feedback to allow you to "catch" problem behaviors before they become a large disruption.	
Self-monitoring	This involves having the student use a clock or timer to monitor his or her focus on a task, wait time for responding, and impulse control. Set short intervals and gradually work to increase time.	
Designate one teacher as adviser	This might involve identifying a former teacher who had success developing rapport and helping student focus attention in class to serve as an advocate. For middle grades and high school students, this might involve having one teacher assume a lead role to collect data on progress across courses and serve as an advocate for the student.	

Table 7.5 Instructional Interventions for Students With ADHD

Instructional Interventions	The purpose of these interventions is to increase engagement in the task by modifying how instruction is delivered to better meet the needs of a child with ADHD.	Strategies That I'd Like to Try/ Strategies That Work for Me
Limit length of lecture	This might include collecting data on how long the student is able to attend and breaking up instruction into a series of minilectures.	
Modify curriculum		
Contextualize tasks	Consider ways to align the curriculum with students' interests. How can you sequence preferred and nonpreferred tasks?	
Introduce novelty	Consider ways to introduce novelty throughout a unit. This might involve saving some new information introduced at the start of a unit for later.	
Increase stimulation	Consider ways of introducing multimodal stimulation. Search Google for images and YouTube for supplementary video and audio.	
Provide choice	Consider ways to provide choice throughout the unit (i.e., topic or format).	
Involve in modeling and/or demonstrating	Consider ways in which verbal instruction may limit students' ability to process information. How can you model or involve the student in modeling instructional content?	

Instructional Interventions	*The purpose of these interventions is to increase engagement in the task by modifying how instruction is delivered to better meet the needs of a child with ADHD.*	Strategies That I'd Like to Try/ Strategies That Work for Me
Modify directions	Short, specific directions; avoid giving multistep directions all at once; check understanding; for activities that require exploration, teachers may need to make additional interpersonal and/or environmental modifications such as increasing physical proximity.	
Provide advanced organizer	This might involve highlighting key points that you can reinforce throughout lesson.	
Modify task		
Titrate challenge	Consider evidence that the task is too challenging or to easy for the student to complete. How can you modify the task to break down the complexity (provide supports) or increase the complexity (remove supports)?	
Evaluate multistep problems	If you cannot be in closer proximity, consider how you can break down tasks into a series of single steps. Consider ways to teach the child how to adapt worksheets one question at a time.	
Break up task length	As with lectures, this can involve breaking up long assignments into a series of shorter tasks and interspersing tasks with breaks, self-correction, or other tasks.	

(Continued)

Table 7.5 (Continued)

Instructional Interventions	*The purpose of these interventions is to increase engagement in the task by modifying how instruction is delivered to better meet the needs of a child with ADHD.*	Strategies That I'd Like to Try/ Strategies That Work for Me
Create procedures for use when stuck	Consider ways to help students cope with impulses that stem from not feeling competent. This might involve integrating a "Please help me" card that quietly signals you that they are struggling.	
Provide self-corrective resources	Consider ways to promote students engaging in self-monitoring and self-correction such as answer keys, audio recording, self-graphing of progress.	
Provide additional one-to-one instruction	Consider ways to use class time, before and after school, and during free periods and the use of support staff and parents to increase your ability to provide student with 1:1 support.	
Provide peer tutoring	Consider ways to introduce peer tutoring	
Provide peer note taker	Consider ways to distribute note-taking responsibilities across the class as a way to provide peer note taking. Consider the benefits to all students of learning how to take notes that a peer can understand	

Table 7.6 Environmental Interventions for Students With ADHD

Environmental Interventions	*The purpose of these interventions is to increase structure in the environment to meet ADHD student's needs for clarity and predictability.*	*Strategies That I'd Like to Try/ Strategies That Work for Me*
Make changes to the physical environment	Consider the physical seams in your instruction. How do students move about the classroom and how can their movement be distracting?	
Evaluate stability of instructional regime	Consider whether more routines and rituals are needed to provide clear expectations and consistency. Consider how often existing routines and rituals are interrupted. How can you develop procedures to support students during interruptions to routines and rituals?	
Specify predictable transition time	Consider developing clear expectations and routines for transition times (i.e., between classes).	
Integrate visual aids	Consider the integration and placement of cues as reminders.	
Reduce noise level	Consider the volume of talk in the classroom. What are ways to reduce the noise level without reducing activity and/or engagement?	

(Continued)

Table 7.6 (Continued)

Environmental Interventions	*The purpose of these interventions is to increase structure in the environment to meet ADHD student's needs for clarity and predictability.*	*Strategies That I'd Like to Try/ Strategies That Work for Me*
Modify seating	Consider implementing preferential seating, seating that is proximal to teacher, to peers that help maintain focus, and away from high traffic, distraction areas.	
Modify desk	Consider the benefits of elevating the student's desk to allow for completing work either seated or standing.	
Color-coded folders	Consider the benefits of introducing color-coded folders to organize work.	
Provide study carrels	Consider the benefits of using folders as provisional study carrels.	
Modify directions	Consider modifying instructions to be short, specific, and avoid giving multiple steps all at once.	

Note: Similar to Lauren's experience with Alex, the research suggests students may perceive increases in the structure of their environment as a form of punishment, so be careful to involve them in designing environmental interventions

Table 7.7 Behavioral Interventions for Students With ADHD

Behavioral Interventions	The purpose of these interventions is to increase the frequency of appropriate behavior while decreasing the frequency of inappropriate behavior through the use of reinforcers or punishments.	Strategies That I'd Like to Try/ Strategies That Work for Me
Time out		
Contracts		
Response costs		
Token economies		
School-home notes		
Self-management		

Note: Franke et al. (2001) found the teachers in their studies did not understand the principles that underlie behavioral interventions and engaged in behaviors that undermined the effectiveness of the intervention. The American Psychological Association has a wonderful resource for teachers interested in learning more about behavioral interventions (http://apa.org/education/k12/classroom-mgmt.aspx)

KEY TERMS

Behavioral interventions: Instructional changes intended to increase a student's appropriate behavior and decrease the student's inappropriate behavior.

Environmental interventions: Instructional changes intended to improve a student's sense of comfort and safety within the classroom environment.

Forethought/planning phase: The first stage of self-regulation; it involves framing the classroom management problem as a task to be accomplished, evaluating the dimensions of the task, and evaluating the available resources that could be used to accomplish the task.

Instructional interventions: Instructional changes intended to increase a student's engagement with the academic or learning tasks of a classroom.

Interpersonal interventions: Instructional changes intended to improve the way a student interacts with others in the classroom.

Performance/monitoring phase: The second stage of self-regulation; it involves implementation of a selected intervention to address the classroom management problem and data collection related to the intervention.

Practical inquiry: The process of systematically observing and reflecting on one's teaching that can lead to self-sustaining generative change.

Productive reflection: Reflection that moves teachers toward improved practice; it typically involves detailed and objective data collection, examination of the data for common threads, a focus on the child's influence on the data, and the development of a plan for future action.

Self-reflection/evaluation phase: The third stage of self-regulation; it involves reflection on the data collected for the chosen intervention and evaluation of the intervention.

Self-regulation: A process that allows teachers to reduce behavior problems and create self-sustaining generative change.

Self-sustaining generative change: A teacher's process of investigating his or her own practice that can lead to the ability to respond flexibly and effectively to new challenges in the classroom.

RESOURCES FOR TEACHERS

Arcia, E., Frank, R., Sánchez-LaCay, A., & Fernáindez, M. C. (2000). Teacher understanding of ADHD as reflected in attributions and classroom strategies. *Journal of Attention Disorders, 4,* 91–101.

Beaty-O'Ferrall, M., Green, A., & Hanna, F. (2010). Classroom management strategies for difficult students: Promoting change through relationships. *Middle School Journal, 41,* 4–11.

Franke, M. L., Carpenter, T., Fennema, E., Ansell, E., & Behrend, J. (1998). Understanding teachers' self-sustaining generative change in the context of professional development. *Teaching and Teacher Education, 14,* 67–80.

Franke, M. L., Carpenter, T. P., Levi, L., & Fennema, E. (2001). Capturing teachers' generative change: A follow-up study of professional development in mathematics. *American Educational Research Journal, 38,* 653–689.

Greene, R. W., Beszterczey, S. K., Katzenstein, T., Park, K., & Goring, J. (2002). Are students with ADHD more stressful to teach? Patterns of stress in an elementary school sample. *Journal of Emotional and Behavioral Disorders, 10,* 79–89.

Jones, V., & Jones, L. (2007). *Comprehensive classroom management: Creating communities of support and problem solving* (8th ed.). Boston, MA: Allyn & Bacon.

Pierangelo, R., & Guiliani, G. (2003). *Classroom management techniques for students with ADHD: A step-by-step guide for educators.* Thousand Oaks, CA: Corwin.

Reid, R. (1999). Attention Deficit Hyperactivity Disorder: Effective methods for the classroom. *Focus on Exceptional Children, 32,* 1. Retrieved from EBSCOhost.

Reif, S. F. (1993). *How to reach and teach children with ADD/ADHD: Practical techniques, strategies, and interventions for helping children with attention problems and hyperactivity.* West Nyack, NY: Center for Applied Research in Education.

Soodak, L. C., & McCarthy, M. R. (2006). Classroom management in inclusive settings. In C. M. Evertson & C. S. Weinstein (Eds.), *Handbook of classroom management* (pp. 461–489). Mahwah, NJ: Lawrence Erlbaum. [On pp. 465–476, the authors review studies of teacher directed, peer mediated, and self-directed interventions]

Zimmerman, B. J. (2004). Becoming a self-regulated learner: An overview. *Theory Into Practice, 41* (2), 64–70.

8

How Can I Improve and Sustain Relationship Quality?

PRODUCTIVE REFLECTION, INTENTIONAL DECISION MAKING, AND TEACHER SELF-CARE

In Chapter 4, we introduced you to Scott and Faith, two middle school teachers who were participating in a yearlong, schoolwide investigation of teacher-student relationships (Davis, 2001b; 2006). You already have a sense of the underlying beliefs that guide Scott's and Faith's interactions with their students. Throughout the course of the year, Scott and Faith were interviewed two additional times. Each time, they were asked to reflect on specific classroom relationships that challenged them and to reflect on why they perceived they were connecting with some students and not connecting with others. We used their class rosters as prompts to ensure they paused to notice each child. Below are excerpts from their systematic reflections on relationship quality.

Acknowledging the Challenges of Sustaining Relationships

Scott

I am always a person who is constantly evaluating and looking back and trying to make sense of things and . . . sometimes I think that if I had to do this again with the same group of students, how would I do things differently? I still haven't come to an answer on that. I can use so many different tactics to try to encourage them and try to teach them something, and if they don't get it then I wonder—Did I not teach it correctly? Or not teach it enough? Or spend too much time on something else? I don't know that there are answers to these questions, but I constantly think about it. I am the person who takes it home. My students, they go home with me every day—figuratively—and they are my life.

What kids need me the most? I think the students that are drawn to me tend to come from homes where they are missing a father figure, and I think being a male teacher automatically draws those, especially boys, to me. I also think those who are struggling with the idea that the arts are not masculine and they see a man participating in the arts and they start questioning. And then I also think those students who have a hard rap, who have been pegged incorrectly, maybe who have been labeled. I have a number of students who have discipline problems in other classes who I will take and who will do well for me. I don't know if it's because of what I expect of them or what I demand of them or my frankness with them—but I get some really tough kids, tough in the respect that they are hard to work with. What kids need me the least? I don't like to talk about those kids. But I guess it's those children who have both parents and come from families that support the arts and they are already in private lessons. They already know what I am teaching. They need less of my attention—but my ego won't let me accept that they don't need me. I feel like I can teach any child, and I feel like I have something to teach every child.

I have a girl in my eighth-period class, Ashawna—she happens to be one of my few African American children. I think because of her race, she is very conscientious of race differences. When a teacher or another student will say things or do things that are a little bit biased, she notices those things and she's very sensitive to those things. And so she's the student I ask about things: "Did this event, was it favoring this student more than that student?" She's my fairness person. If she's disruptive, then I have go home and think about that because chances are I was wrong. If she had the courage to say something and she would stand up in front of a class and do that. . . . It would definitely be something that caught my attention, and I would have to put some stock into whatever she was doing or saying.

I think that a bad relationship would be one in which damaging things are said and done. I think it happens when a child is just totally belligerent and constantly makes remarks that are inappropriate or does things that are disruptive, and they just almost seem unreachable. In my high school class, there is a student whom I had never taught before and was very disruptive the first class. Again, it was an African American female—but totally different from Ashawna. This child is argumentative and defensive; she resents any type of authority—especially White male authority—and she does disrupt frequently. And it is very difficult because even when I call on her, she becomes argumentative in front of the class. She is very difficult and I'm not sure that I've connected with her. I don't know if this is a good analogy, but there are some children that are just beautiful children because of their personalities and their attitudes and abilities to cooperate. This child, she is unattractive because of her attitude. I'll be fair to her, but I'm probably not going to treat her the same way that I would treat Ashawna if she disrupted class. I'm sure that makes some people scream about fairness, but I think to treat every child the same *is* unfair. Ashawna doesn't need a lot of supervision. She's very self-motivated, self-disciplined. This other student, she needs a lot of discipline and supervision. . . . It's about teaching them responsibility, teaching them accountability; about learning that if I want to do this activity, I have to *earn* it. You don't just get a handout—you need to contribute to the effort.

Ultimately, the students have control. I tell them this all the time. I can't make you do anything. I can make a request. I can encourage you to do it. If you choose to comply, then you are saying you are putting someone else before yourself and you are being unselfish. If you decide you are not going to comply and you are going to disrupt, you are saying that you are more important than everything else that is going on.

Faith

My goals are a little bit different from others, but my class is a little bit different from others. I want my students to be prepared for high school. I want them to be where they will *want* to stay in school and finish. I want them to have a successful year and *legitimately* pass. They're so used to failing. . . . I also think the system can lose credibility. You know they just have to respect the system itself, almost. They just have to come in and, you know, just *know* that this is what we do at school. And I think, sometimes they begin to feel like the system isn't doing what it is supposed to be doing. They get fed up.

What kids need me the most? This boy [pointing to a name on her roster], he needs a mother figure, the attention, the approval. He constantly wants to chitchat with me—not necessarily about school or work—just anything. There are several of them that are kind of needy in that way. They just seem to want a lot of approval and attention. Everything is, "Look at my work. How is this? Is it alright?" And this girl [pointing to another name on the roster], I think she asks for approval in different ways. She acts very eager to please and is clingy in different ways. She wants to literally be nearer to me and tell me about things that are happening to her. What students need me the least? This boy—I think he has a good home situation; he seems well adjusted. And there are several in that situation [pointing to more names]. And there are kids who are recovering. This girl, she lost her mother last year, and I didn't know how that would change her, how it would affect her. But she seems to have adjusted. When things like that happen, children can fall to pieces, but she seems to have held together in spite of it all. What's happening at home really affects how much they need from me. You know, when they act out in class it's not because they are bad kids; they just want or need something. Or they just *can't* do what they are supposed to do, and they get so frustrated, and they have to find another way to express themselves and get attention.

When things go wrong, I always try talking to the students first. I just pull them out to have a little private conference and say, "Things seemed to have changed. What's going on with you?" and a lot of times that seems to be enough. I mean, I can be in a bad mood too. Sometimes, something that is small, you know, just rubs you the wrong way and you just go off on them a little bit more than normally. And I'll regret it. I just say, "You know, I'm sorry. That was more than you actually deserved." And they're very forgiving. You have to remember, these are children. Hopefully, that will keep you from losing it. But I think it's normal to feel angry. With thirty kids at a time, there's no way everybody's doing what they're supposed to all the time. And it can escalate when you've just told this kid for the fiftieth time to please be quiet. You're helping one kid while another is across the room distracting others. Yeah, it can make you angry.

Some kids, however, when you ask what's wrong they will tell you, "Because you don't like me. You're not fair. Everyone is on my case." They throw it back on you. Others will say, "I don't know," and they go back in the room and continue to act out. I try by saying, "Well, give me an example. How do I treat you differently?" There was a boy I had a couple of years ago who just *hated* me, and before it was over, I didn't feel too good about him either. It was a real hard relationship. Every day it would escalate and I would think, "OK, today, I'm not gonna get pulled into it." I dreaded every single day. That was the worst year ever. And we could never get his parents here for a conference. It was a sad home situation for him too.

I think another conflict I have is that there is more and more accountability, and by teaching the SUCCESS class, when the scores come in, I'm not going to look good at all. Most of them, last year, were in the single-digit percentiles. We'll improve, yes. But comparatively my students' scores aren't going to look good. And I really enjoy it, you know. I love these kids, and they really do need something from me. They need some success and *not* to make a 50% each time they take a test or turn in an assignment. I feel useful in this role—but the system *needs* to be doing more for kids like this. Kids who haven't been outside of our county, who don't have telephones in their homes—much less computers. And their parents are similar—many cannot read or spell. In a perfect world, everyone has an average or above IQ and average home life. But my world is not perfect.

Note: Cases reconstructed from Davis, 2001b; see also Davis, 2006.

UNDERSTANDING TEACHER NEEDS FOR AUTONOMY, COMPETENCE, AND CONNECTION

In Chapter 2 we argued students' (mis)behavior in the classroom may emerge as a function of their attempts to meet their needs to feel competent, autonomous, and related to themselves, their teachers, and their peers (see Chapter 1). As teachers, we also share these needs: (a) to feel competent about our work in the classroom, (b) to feel autonomous in our decision making, and (c) to feel connected to our colleagues and our students. As adults we have more arenas (i.e., both in school and in our personal lives) and more skills to meet these needs. Often, however, we overlook our own needs and may seek to meet our needs for competence, autonomy, and connection with our students. It is not an unreasonable expectation to seek meeting our own needs for competence in the work our students complete, to meet our needs for autonomy through our instructional and management decisions, and to meet our connection needs through our interactions with our students. However, in vertical relationships—where teachers have both administrative and evaluative power—we have to be conscious of the potential to be engaged in a dual relationship with a student (Richmond & Padgett, 2002). **Dual relationships** happen when teachers move beyond an impersonal, professional relationship (Newberry & Davis, 2008, p. 1973) with students to more personal relationships—relationships where teachers create less rigid interpersonal **boundaries**. In professional relationships teachers strive for "separation from my work life and personal life" (Richmond & Padgett, 2002, p. 59). In dual relationships, teachers may take on additional roles: providing snacks and supplies; disclosing personal information (e.g., about their own schooling and families) to build rapport; volunteering additional hours to tutor, mentor, or create extracurricular opportunities; or comforting and counseling in a time of crisis.

The literature is replete with examples of exemplary teachers who assumed additional roles to support their students. The challenge with entering into a dual relationship with students and colleagues is that they can leave us open to feeling depleted, burned out. As teachers, we need to set boundaries to both maintain the focus on the shared learning goals of the class and to protect ourselves from becoming burned out and incapable of serving our students. On the other hand, when setting boundaries, we can fall victim to the larger discourses we discussed in Chapter 6 and establish boundaries that privilege some relationships and marginalize others.

In their study of teacher **boundary setting**, Aultman and colleagues (2009) found that teachers set boundaries that were *institutional* (e.g., How closely will I adhere to each school policy?), *intellectual* (e.g., What curricula will I teach and how? Where does my expertise end?), *interpersonal* (e.g., What kinds of relationships will I cultivate with students, parents, colleagues? How will I communicate with students, parents, colleagues? How will I wield my power as a teacher?), *cultural* (e.g., To what extent am I willing to incorporate values and norms from another culture into my classroom?), and *personal* (e.g., To what extent will I sacrifice my personal life to meet professional demands?). Determining where to draw the line can be challenging. In our study of tough decision making, experienced teachers weighted the relative potential risks *to* the student and to their professional identity as well as the potential risks to society. (Andrzejewksi & Davis, 2008). In analyzing their responses, we realized that perhaps more important than the actual decisions for where to draw the line were the conversations our teachers were (and were not) having with their colleagues and administrators (and us) about developing deliberate decision rules for how and when to set boundaries. Teachers who had devoted time to identifying their personal boundaries (given the context in which they taught) felt more satisfied with their jobs and more confident about their pedagogy.

How were Scott and Faith's needs for autonomy, competence, and connection challenged by their students?

What types of boundaries are Scott and Faith struggling to set with their students?

In what ways are their conflicts with students a reflection of unclear boundaries?

SYSTEMATICALLY REFLECTING
ON RELATIONSHIP QUALITY

In Chapter 2, we provided tools for reflecting on management structures and classroom climate. The routines, rituals, and structures we establish in our classroom can go a long way to developing and maintaining warm and productive relationships with students. However, classrooms are diverse places and children are in varying phases of acquiring cognitive and social skills (Davis, 2009) and may be less skilled in the work of relationships (Davis, 2003). In a meta-analysis of over 100 studies, Marzano and colleagues (2003) found that teachers who had high-quality relationships with their students reported 31% fewer behavior problems in their classroom over the course of an academic year. As with Scott and Faith, students with uninviting behaviors, however, can not only disrupt the academic flow of a classroom but can undermine the climate of the classroom and our ability to cultivate productive relationships with the other students in the class.

How Do We Cultivate Relationships
With Uninviting Students?

Several studies have documented the benefits of systematically reflecting on relationship quality with students. Consider the process in Chapter 7 that Lauren used for identifying strategies to promote Alex's engagement in class. The same principles of **productive reflection** can be employed to improve relationship quality with uninviting students. When systematically reflecting on relationship quality, the goal is to identify the relationships in which you, as the teacher, feel distant or alienated, unwanted, or not needed. These feelings can fester and result in our expressing excessive negative emotions or engaging in our own distancing behaviors. When we acknowledge that we do not feel as connected to some students in the class, we can then consider the sources of those feelings. Is it because the student holds vastly different interests? Is it because the student engages in behaviors we perceive as disrespectful?

In Chapter 2, we provided tools for systematic reflection on classroom organization and climate. Davis (2006) found teachers were more systematic in their reflections on relationship quality when they used a class roster to methodically consider each child in their class. She asked teachers to consider (a) which students they felt like they had or had not connected with and (b) which students they perceived needed or did not need them. Several studies have employed a measure called the Inclusion of the Other in the Self (Aron, Aron, & Smollan, 1992) to examine teachers' feelings of closeness and **influence** (Davis, Gableman, & Wingfield, 2011; Newberry, 2010; Newberry & Davis, 2008; Straub & Davis, 2006). These studies consistently indicate that teachers' feelings of distance or lack of influence affect their motivations to engage both interpersonally and academically with students.

Once you have explored your own feelings about the relationship, you can gather data you need to improve the relationship (see Chapter 7). What do you need to know about a student's past relationships with teachers? Beaty-O'Ferrall, Green, and Hanna (2010) argued that when working with uninviting students, teachers need to empathize with students and cultivate feelings of compassion. **Empathy** is defined as "seeing with eyes of another, hearing with eyes of another, and feeling with heart of another" (Adler, 1956, p. 135, as cited in Beaty-O'Ferrall et al., 2010). Once we have developed empathy for our students, then we can begin to reframe our understandings of uninviting behavior and develop more adaptive patterns of interacting with students.

> Both Scott and Faith conceived of their influence on students as something distinct from their ability to control students.
>
> In what ways do you attempt to influence your students without trying to control them?

SELF-COMPOSURE: UNDERSTANDING THE DIFFERENCE BETWEEN RESPONDING AND REACTING

Developmental approaches to classroom discipline often reflect an understanding of attachment theory and the ways in which children develop working models of adult-child relationships (Watson & Ecken, 2003). Central to an attachment perspective on student-teacher relationships is the belief that students bring to the classroom schemas, or models, about the nature of their social world and of social relationships. Attachment theory describes the ways in which children come to trust adults as a function of how frequently and warmly parents respond to their demands. Parental relationships then create lenses used by children to interpret future relationships with nonparental adults. Children who experience insecurity in their parental relationships often experience direct exertions of parental authority in addition to harsh or unpredictable responses from their parents to their demands. From this perspective, when teachers attempt to control students' (mis)behavior through the use of rewards or consequences, it can result in exacerbating problems in the teacher-student relationship because it confirms insecurely attached children's worldview that the world does not respond to their needs or will respond in a harsh controlling manner.

It is important to remember, however, that the process of bonding with students is more complex than simply responding with warmth. Not all students are inviting of relationships or easy to interact with. Any parent who has had a colicky baby knows the challenge of responding with warmth to an infant who pushes away from you and screams for hours. When children enter school, they enter with their own motivations, values, and skills for relationships with teachers that can move them toward relationships with teachers, move them away from relationships with teachers, or move them toward conflict with teachers (Birch & Ladd, 1997; Ladd, Birch, & Buhs, 1999). The reality is that some relationships in the classroom will feel uninviting because they require us to actively pursue students who withdraw from us, or they require us to manage emotions that emerge during conflict and are often intense.

To develop relationships with uninviting students, we may need to retrain our natural way of interpreting conflict in the classroom. Social psychologist Mark Leary (2004) argued that we are "wired" to monitor our environment for clues that we are not being accepted. When we receive them, we feel hurt and we have instinctual responses to feeling hurt: Sometimes we want to strike back and hurt the other person, sometimes we want to give in, sometimes we want to break away, and sometimes we simply shut down. It is hard to imagine that we could feel hurt by the things students say and do, but subtle resistances to our attempts to cultivate relationships with and among them and to the curriculum we so carefully planned can be interpreted as a form of rejection.

Early studies of teacher-student conflict found teachers can misconstrue students' exuberance for hostility or their silent respect for sullen resistance (Hargreaves, 1998). These judgments, in turn, can affect the emotions we experience as teachers and the extent to which we enact caring behaviors. For example, Jere Brophy and Mary McCaslin (1992) found when teachers interpreted the source of behavior problems as a lack of competence rather than a student's attempt to usurp control in the class, they tended to respond with more caring. It is important to remember that our perception of what is happening in our classroom may not be calibrated with our students' perceptions. One misinterpretation need not define a relationship. However, when students and teachers repeatedly label each others' behavior as the result of some stable, internal characteristic that lies outside of their control (Weiner, 2000, 2007), discrete feelings of disrespect can become more global judgments of students as disrespectful and teachers as mean. Assuming a deficit perspective on a relationship with a student (i.e., a student imbues an inherent shortfall) can lead to teachers changing, and in fact lowering, their standards for student performance and the quality of their instruction (Ford & Grantham, 2003).

It is important to remember, that students (mis)behave for a variety of predictable cognitive and social reasons. Younger children, in particular, may violate our norms for behavior simply because they either have not acquired the norm (i.e., they don't know how to behave), or they have not learned how to coordinate a variety of norms (i.e., they can't figure out how to control their behavior around their friends). As we mentioned earlier, students may (mis)behave because they are trying to meet an unmet emotional need: the need for attention, for love, for competence, or for control. And children and adolescents also may (mis)behave when there is a lack of congruence between behavioral expectations at home and school or simply because students are testing our limits or boundaries to learn more about their world and us. Watson and Ecken (2003) provide several recommendations that are positive examples of teacher responses (see Figure 8.1).

Children and adolescents rarely intend to hurt, frustrate, or offend their teachers. When dealing with uninviting or disruptive behavior, we first need to figure out how to get ourselves composed (Chang & Davis, 2009). What does it mean to be composed? **Composure** involves moving to a state of calm, self-control—a place where we can respond to students productively:

> Learning to express strong emotions, like anger and frustration, respectfully and selectively is a learned behavior. You don't have to be a victim of your emotions. You can choose your response. You don't have to react. And as you make those choices, your children are watching and listening. You are their role model, teaching them with your words and actions what adults do when faced with a rush of powerful emotions. (Kurcinka, 2000, p. 37)

Often, our instinctual reactions to avoid children who are uninviting, to confront children who are disrespectful, or to control misbehavior with reward or consequences result in reinforcing the exact behaviors we are trying to eliminate.

Figure 8.1	Recommendations for Responding to Problem Behavior When Teaching and Reminding Students Is Not Enough

- Encourage students to feel empathy and, if necessary, help them think of ways to make reparations for the harm they have caused.
- Encourage and give students time to think about the causes of their actions, and challenge their efforts to blame others for their own misdeeds.
- Assume that students want to behave well, and remind them or redirect them in a spirit of helpfulness.
- When students don't change their behavior following a helpful reminder, consider ignoring the behavior if further action would be more disruptive. Other possible actions are reassessing the situation, directing students to a quiet place for reflection, discussing the situation with a student at a later time, and reaffirming your commitment to them.
- For extremely volatile students or in a situation that feels out of control, seek help—for example from the school psychologist, principal, or special education teacher.
- If it's necessary to ask students to leave the room, consider preparing meaningful work for them to do while out of the classroom.
- Be sure to reconnect with students when they return and discuss ways to make it possible for them to remain in control and in the classroom.
- Prepare students for substitutes and student teachers. Remember they have come to depend on your support to cope with classroom challenges.
- Hold a class meeting after the class has had a substitute or student teacher to discuss successes and rough spots.

Source: Watson & Ecken (2003, p. 184).

Solving relational problems, connecting with uninviting children, requires us to deploy our own critical-thinking and problem-solving skills. When we model gaining composure over our emotions, we model the difference between mindlessly reacting to our environment and meaningfully responding to individuals.

Gaining composure can involve active relaxation techniques (e.g., taking a deep breath, shaking it off) or it can involve taking a break (e.g., having the student sit in a safe, quiet place). It is from a stance of **self-composure** that we can use interpersonal conflict with a student as an opportunity to teach new skills. When we help students to understand interpersonal conflict, we develop their abilities to be better problem solvers. During conflicts, we learn that others have had different experiences from us, that they see the world differently, and that they use different strategies to feel safe. From a stance of self-composure, we can help students learn that feelings change; anger can be resolved, and hurt feeling mended. And we can help children learn how to teach others how they want to be treated. From a stance of self-composure, we can teach children those words they need to talk to adults and peers, how to speak in a tone of voice that is assertive not aggressive, and how to accomplish their goals in appropriate ways.

INTERRUPTING CYCLES OF RELATIONSHIP CONFLICT

Gaining self-composure is merely the first step in developing adaptive patterns of interacting with uninviting students. Part of retraining our natural ways of interpreting conflict with students is learning to act in a way that projects the kind of relationship we want to have with them. In the following section we offer strategies that consistently surface in the literature for improving problematic relationships.

Positive Intent

Once we have gained self-composure, it is important to reappraise students' behavioral transgressions as unintentional mistakes. When we view (mis)behavior as a mistake, we create opportunities for teaching and learning. We express empathy when we remember that students want to feel competent in school, want to feel autonomous and in control of their behavior, and fundamentally want to be connected to their classmates and to their teacher. Bailey (2000; see also Chang & Davis, 2009) argued that teachers' develop predictable *trigger thoughts*, or less adaptive ways of judging student behavior, that hinder in our abilities to offer **positive intent** to students. Trigger thoughts often magnify situations and make them appear more unstable and problematic than they really are (see Chapter 6 discussion of positive intent and trigger thoughts).

It is important to keep in mind that uninviting behavior often reflects students' attempts to protect themselves from a real or perceived hurt they are about to experience. Watson and Ecken (2003) argued that it is really important to resist the urge to be punitive: "Seriously misbehaving students in her classroom had experienced plenty of punishment in their young lives and . . . it had neither helped them become caring and responsible nor had it kindled their love of learning" (p. 158). As we mentioned in Chapter 4, we can adopt a non-judgmental, nonblaming stance by noticing behavior that doesn't work for us: "I have a problem," or "This behavior doesn't work for me." We can then offer students positive intent: "I know that you want to be successful in this class." "I realize that you need to feel in control of your learning."

> Consider Scott's approach to Ashwana.
> What are the barriers to his offering positive
> intent to other students?

Private Signals for Problem Behaviors

Part of offering positive intent is believing that uninviting students *want* to change their behavior. Watson and Ecken (2003) reminded us that the goal is to work in partnership with our students to develop more adaptive ways of interacting. It is important to remember that changing our patterns of interacting with others is difficult work. Students will need support including subtle reminders and cues to prevent and cope with (mis)behavior. Consider how you can create a verbal or nonverbal system that alerts students to the fact that you notice they are engaging or about to engage in a problem behavior. Reeve (2006) referred to the private signals and attempts to redirect students as **gentle discipline**.

Modeling and Facilitating Relationship Repair

Students need to understand that classrooms are places that are safe from harm including physical, emotional, and social. However, as we learned in Chapter 4, conflict is a natural by-product of learning to interact with someone who is different from you. Therefore classrooms need to be places where we model for students how to repair relationships; this includes acknowledging when we misinterpreted their intentions, when we lost our temper, or even when we forgot to follow through on our commitments.

Coping in the Moment With Harm

What can we do when one student's misbehavior results in harming another student in the classroom, or in harming us? When students harm each other or their teachers, we can use that situation as an opportunity to teach them how to take another's perspective, to help them develop empathy and compassion for another person, to help them to understand the obligations we have to the people in our community to treat them with respect and dignity, and to provide them with an opportunity to repair the relationship.

When something hurtful happens in the classroom, we must begin by remembering that students need time to work on reducing the intensity of their emotions. It is important to teach students that they can be in control of their own emotions—that they can become self-composed. When harm happens, students may need space away from you or from each other. Finding safe places in your classroom or with another colleague for them to gain composure is critical.

When something hurtful happens in the classroom, we also need to remember that uninviting students often need reassurance that, despite their behavior, they belong in the classroom.

Once she got control of her own emotional response, [she was able to] provide her students with a very deep kind of reassurance—the reassurance that she still cared about them and was not going to punish or desert them, even though they had done something really bad. (Watson & Ecken, 2003, p. 142)

Teachers can model productive relationships by reminding uninviting students that we all forget, we all make mistakes, and we often hurt people we care about— but we do not have to be defined by those moments (Davis, 2006).

When something hurtful happens in the classroom, students also need time to think about how to make it better. We often want students to make amends on our timetable. However, processing why a conflict happened can not only take children and adolescents longer than adults but may also require some support to think through the situation. And teachers need to remember that students are not always capable of identifying how to repair a relationship with them or their peers. They may need ideas for how to respond and specific words to say.

Modeling Restitution

Watson and Ecken (2003) argued that in caring communities when we harm one another, we have an obligation to repair the harm we have done. Sometimes accepting responsibility and saying that we are sorry is not enough. We model restitution by choosing to engage in behaviors that amend the situation. **Restitution** provides children with an opportunity to learn that they can change how they see themselves and how others see them. Acts of restitution can involve fixing things that were broken, following through with a commitment, or providing help.

> In what ways does Faith model restitution with her students?

Coping With Intense
or Persistent Misbehavior

What happens when you feel like you have tried everything? You have devoted time to reflecting productively on how to modify the design and structure of your classroom to meet his or her individual needs (see Chapter 7), and you have devoted time to reflecting productively on how to improve your patterns of interacting with students. Nothing seems to work. In 1977, Glasser (1977) developed a multistep process for coping with persistent misbehavior. Because it somewhat depersonalizes the interactions you have with a student, it is important to remember this framework is "meant for use with students who persistently violate rules that are reasonable and are administered fairly by teachers who maintain a positive, problem solving stance" (Brophy, 2006, p. 35).

When updating these steps (see Figure 8.2), Brophy emphasized the importance of Step 7: following up with relationship repair. Even in the face of persistent misbehavior, as teachers we need to reassure students about our deep understanding of their goodness and our desire for them to be a part of the classroom. As Faith reflected in Chapter 2, because our students' behavior may not improve during the year we are with them, we may not realize how our consistency and reassurance contributes to positive change in the long term. "You know, sometimes the dreaded student, they'll come back years later and they've just matured and everything is going fine. It wasn't as hopeless as you thought."

Emotional Labor and Compassion Fatigue

To care for students requires a great deal of emotional understanding and emotional management, often referred to as emotional labor (Hargreaves, 1998). It can take months to develop productive relationships with uninviting students (Watson & Ecken, 2003). To end here would fail to acknowledge a tension in the caring teacher literature in that teachers who care more may be more prone to feeling emotional

Figure 8.2	Steps for Addressing Persistent Behavior Problems

Step 1. List your typical reactions to student's disruptive behavior.

Step 2. Analyze the list to see what techniques do or do not work and resolve not to repeat the latter.

Step 3. Improve your relationship with the student by providing additional encouragement, asking the student to perform special errands, showing concern, or implying that things will improve.

Step 4. Focus the student's attention on the disruptive behavior by requiring the student to describe what he or she has been doing. Be sure the student describes the behavior accurately. Then, ask the student to stop engaging in the behavior.

Step 5. If the disruptive behavior continues, call a short conference, and again have the student describe the behavior. Then have the student state whether the behavior is against the rules or recognized expectations, and ask what he or she should be doing instead.

Step 6. If necessary, repeat Step 5, but this time add that the student will have to formulate a plan to solve the problem. This plan must be more than a simple agreement to stop the behavior. It must include a commitment to positive actions designed to eliminate the behavior.

Step 7. If the problem persists, isolate the student from the class until he or she has devised a plan for ensuring that the rules will be followed in the future, gotten the plan approved, and made a commitment to follow it. Attempt to repair the relationship when the intensity has subsided.

Step 8. If it doesn't work, the next step is in-school suspension. Now the student must deal with the principal or someone other than the teacher, but this person will repeat Step 5.

Step 9. If the student remains out of control or does not comply with in-school suspension rules, the student's parents are called to take him or her home for the day, and the student resumes in-school suspension the next day.

Step 10. Students who do not respond to the previous steps are removed from school and referred to another agency.

Source: Glasser (1977); updated by Brophy (2006, pp. 35–36).

exhaustion, to becoming burnt out and to leaving the field. Initially studied among service workers, **emotional labor** was defined as the experience of employees when they are required to feel, or at least project the appearance of, certain emotions as they engage in job-relevant interactions (Hochschild, 1979, 1983). Early findings showed that when employees were required to display an emotion (e.g., compassion) that was inconsistent with what they were really feeling (e.g., anger) they were more prone to becoming emotionally exhausted. Emotional labor can also involve being aware that you are consciously trying to change your emotions or actively trying to fake feeling or expressing an emotion that you know is more appropriate. This type of suppression can occur when interacting with challenging students. When studying labor in other service professions (e.g., social work), researchers have found emotional labor also predicts feeling burnout and attrition from the field (Chang & Davis, 2009).

Alas, we view emotional labor as an inherent component of teacher-student relationships. This is because, as teachers, we serve a socializing role. We help students interpret and understand their own emotions, the emotion rules for different social and academic situations, and we provide them with opportunities to practice monitoring and managing their emotions (Thompson, 1990, 1991). Students, however, are in varying phases of acquiring cognitive and social skills and may be less skilled in the work of relationships. Even as they age, the task of helping children to regulate their emotion experiences and emotion displays becomes no less complex for teachers of preadolescents and adolescents. Though students in middle and high school are likely to be more adept at identifying their own emotions and are likely to have acquired knowledge about display rules, in a single day middle grades and high school teachers may encounter more than a hundred students who are struggling with their own emotion management. And as if this were not enough, as teachers we are asked to develop our relationships with students en mass. Our expression and nonexpression of emotions occurs in a shared space where one interaction may be observed or discussed by the other students in the class. It is for this reason that teaching requires tremendous amounts of energy to *know* what we feel, *why* we feel it, and *what* are our underlying goals for expressing or not expressing an emotion for an individual student as well as to the class (Chang & Davis, 2009).

Compassion Fatigue

It is important to remember that to be a caring teacher, we need to identify ways to care for ourselves (Ben-Ze'ev, 2000). This involves learning how to create healthy intellectual and interpersonal boundaries and to identify sources of support that we can employ when the task of caring for a student, or a group of students, is beyond our resources. A critical element of adaptive coping with disruptive behavior involves knowing when to seek help. Compassion is an emotion we experience when we perceive that we understand the depth of another's suffering combined with the desire to alleviate it. In the field of social work, Figley and colleagues (Figley, 1995; Radley & Figley, 2007) argued that the experience of compassion is essential in order to be able to develop rapport and empathize with clients. Are teachers at risk for compassion fatigue? We believe so. Empathizing with children who are experiencing crisis in their lives brings with it certain risks for teachers. Consider this statement from Perry (2003):

> All too often the adults are working in difficult, resource-limited situations. The children may present with a host of problems that can confuse or overwhelm their caregivers and treaters. The pain and helplessness of these children can be passed on to those around them. . . . [T]rying to work in a complicated, frustrating and often "insensitive" system, feeling helpless when trying to heal these children—all can make the adults working with these children vulnerable to develop their own emotional or behavioral problems. (p. 2)

Compassion fatigue happens when teachers take on their students' problems; become mentally, physically, and/or emotionally exhausted; and develop feelings of hopelessness and disconnection from their students and colleagues. Teachers experiencing compassion fatigue may question their effectiveness as helpers and doubt their purpose as teachers. Compassion fatigue can come on quickly and with little warning. It can be the result of exposure to a single traumatic interaction with a student or as a reaction to one intensely disruptive relationship. Five factors have been noted as contributing to compassion fatigue:

1. Poor self-care

2. Previous unresolved trauma (e.g., with former student)

3. Inability or refusal to control work stressors

4. A lack of satisfaction at work

5. High levels of suppressing stressful emotions (e.g., anger, frustration)

We believe teachers need to monitor for symptoms of compassion fatigue; know your stress cues. Are you the kind of person that becomes impatient with students when you are stressed? Do you begin sounding like a drill sergeant? No matter how hard you promise yourself at the start of the day that you will not yell, do you find yourself yelling by the end of the day? Monitoring these feelings and behaviors can allow you to seek the support and care you need to feel compassion for your most challenging students. Ultimately, we are on the frontline of service for our students who face challenging circumstances in their communities and families. However challenging it may be to interact with students in crisis, they need our support the most. Without compassion, problem students are likely to become alienated from their teachers (Finn, 1989) and feel less motivated in school (Cornelius-White, 2008). We hope teachers experiencing compassion fatigue will seek the support they need, both within the school and in their personal lives, to care for themselves so that they remain compassionate and continue to serve children in need.

Parker J. Palmer (1998) once wrote about his experiences teaching the "student from hell" (p. 43). He described being sucked into myopia and becoming shortsighted about his instruction and impact on students because he found himself focusing too much on the relationships that were problematic. He lost his center and found it difficult to look beyond his failures to connect. After the class was finished, the student serendipitously approached him and said it had been one of his best classes; then Palmer remembered that it is often hard to ascertain our impact in the moment, that our initial impressions can say more about us than about the student. Devoting time to reflecting on our classroom relationships often enables us to get out of the myopia and realize what *is* working in our classroom. Devoting time to reflecting on our classroom relationships is a form of self-care, permitting us space to acknowledge the struggles we all face as teachers to connect with uninviting students. Devoting time to reflecting on classroom relationships enables us to gain perspective on the factors that contribute to relationship conflict, to approach challenging relationships feeling calm and composed, and to model for students the appropriate way to build and sustain relationships.

CONNECT TO YOUR PRACTICE

Identify Your Trigger Thoughts

Chang and Davis (2009) and Bailey (2000) argued that relationships with students can turn sour when we get in to a pattern of judging student (mis)behavior that magnifies the problem and/or assume our students intend to defy our authority. Bailey (2000, p. 31) created a checklist of trigger thoughts, or thoughts that can distort a situation, making a situation seem more problematic than it is (see Figure 8.3).

For this exercise, think of a particular student with whom you felt the relationship was characterized by a lot of conflict and where you often felt angry or hopeless. Read the following trigger thoughts. Put a check mark next to the ones that sound familiar to you and may contribute to your angry/hopeless response.

Figure 8.3	Trigger Thought Checklist

Assumed Intent

_____ He or she is just doing that to annoy me.

_____ He or she is deliberately trying to defy me.

_____ He or she is trying to drive me crazy.

_____ He or she is trying to push my buttons.

_____ He or she is trying to intentionally tune me out.

_____ He or she is trying to embarrass me.

_____ He or she is trying to wear me down so I'll give in.

_____ He or she is trying to manipulate me.

_____   [Your Trigger]

_____   [Your Trigger]

Magnification

_____ I can't stand this one minute longer!

_____ This behavior is intolerable!

_____ He or she has gone too far this time!

_____ He or she never listens!

_____ He or she never stays on task!

_____ How dare he or she speak to me that way!

_____ He or she turns everything into a power struggle!

_____ This is a nightmare!

_____ [Your Trigger]

_____ [Your Trigger]

Labeling

_____ This is getting out of control.

_____ This is just plain manipulation.

_____ He or she is lazy.

_____ He or she is stubborn.

_____ He or she is disrespectful.

_____ He or she is ungrateful.

_____ He or she doesn't care about anyone but himself.

_____ He or she is a mean/cruel kid.

_____ He or she is such a smart mouth.

_____ [Your Trigger]

_____ [Your Trigger]

Source: Bailey (2000, p. 31).

CONNECT TO YOUR PRACTICE

Systematically Reflect on Student Relationship Quality

In this chapter, we argue teachers can feel empowered to improve their relationships with (and among) students when they take the time to systematically reflect on the quality of their relationships. As with the Davis ((2001b, 2006) research, this can simply be accomplished using a class roster and pushing yourself to reflect on your feelings of connection with each student.

In 2006, Melissa Newberry and I developed a protocol based on *The Inclusion of the Other in the Self Scale* (IOS, see Aron, Aron, & Smollan, 1992; see Newberry & Davis, 2008). The IOS is a set of nonverbal scales. For exploring closeness, two circles of the same size are used to represent the two individuals in the relationship. Melissa prepared a set of circles for each student in the class; one circle had the student's first name on it, and the other said *me* to represent the teacher. The teachers were asked to place the circles on a line to indicate how close or distant they felt to each student in their class. Melissa carefully recorded the placement of the circles and the teachers' rationales for their feelings. After rating the entire class, Melissa asked each teacher to organize the sets to range from closest to most distant and to reflect on any patterns they saw (see Figure 8.4).

Teachers in our studies also rated a subset of their classroom relationships for how much influence they felt they had with each student (see Davis et al., 2011; Newberry & Davis, 2008). For exploring influence, five circles of increasing size are used to represent the amount of influence an individual has. The circles of increasing size represented the teacher. Teachers were asked to pick a size (from smallest to largest) to represent how much influence they perceived they had over each student (see Figure 8.5).

Templates for completing this activity follow. Thus, to complete this structured reflection, you would need to take these steps:

1. Copy the rating template so that you have one rating scale for each child in your class.

2. Push yourself to *list a rationale* for why you feel this way about each student or why you perceive this level of influence for each student.

3. Cut and sort the ratings from closest to most distant OR from most influence to least influence.
   a. What patterns do you notice in terms of the students?
   b. What patterns do you notice in terms of your rationales?

4. Make a plan of action. Identify a group of students with whom you would like to improve your relationship. Use what you learned from your ratings, rationales, and organization to identify some strategies you could implement for improving relationship quality.

5. After a period of time, repeat the activity. What has changed? What has not?

Figure 8.4   Measure of Feelings of Closeness

Student Name: _____

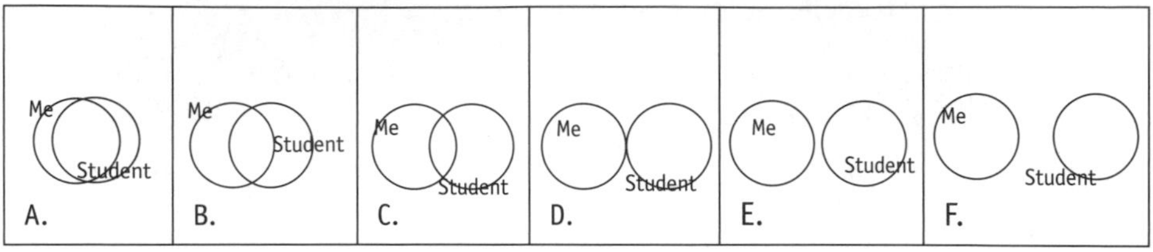

A.   B.   C.   D.   E.   F.

Rationale: _____
_____

Student Name: _____

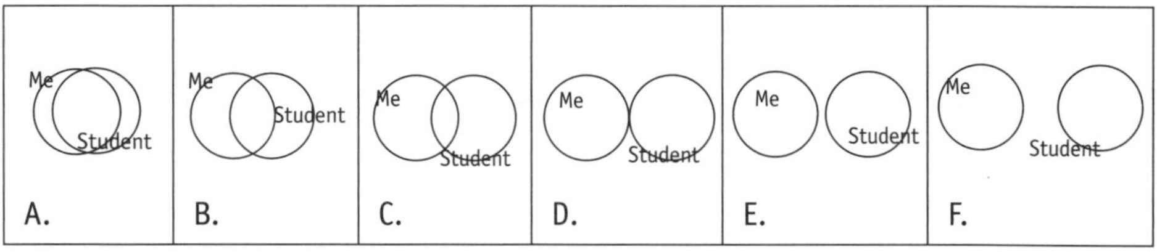

A.   B.   C.   D.   E.   F.

Rationale: _____
_____

Student Name: _____

A.   B.   C.   D.   E.   F.

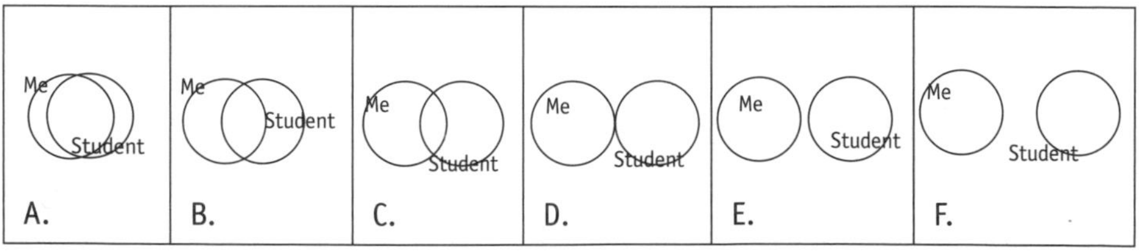

Rationale: _____
_____

Source: Aron et al. (1992)

Figure 8.5 Measure of Influence

Student Name: _____

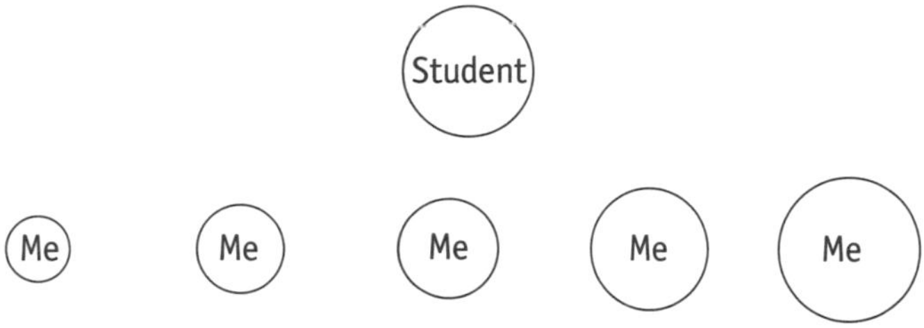

Student

Me   Me   Me   Me   Me

Rationale: _____

Student Name: _____

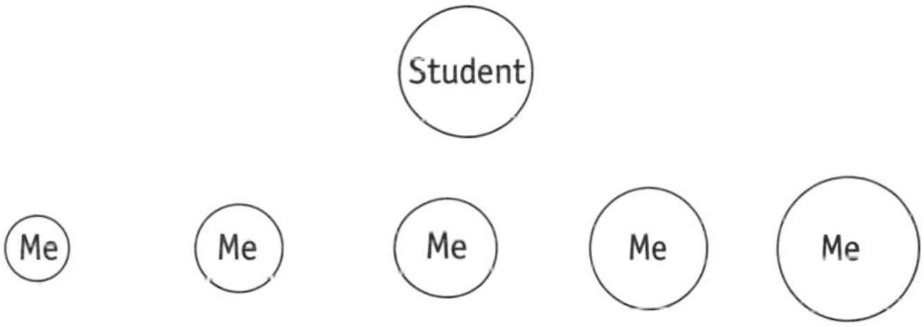

Student

Me   Me   Me   Me   Me

Rationale: _____
_____

Source: Aron et al. (1992)

CONNECT TO YOUR PRACTICE

Guide for Productive Reflection on Relationship Conflict

We recognize that for teachers who see multiple classes of students throughout an academic day, systematic reflections using class rosters may produce an overwhelming amount of information to organize, synthesize, and interpret. Below, we offer prompts to support productive reflection (E. A. Davis, 2006) on relationship conflict.

Describe the Incident. *Remember to describe the incident with as much specificity and accuracy as possible. Avoid using colloquial phrases and adjectives that are vague.*

Connect It to Other Incidents. *Again, try to describe other incidents with as much specificity and accuracy as possible. Dates and times may be important.*

Draw Connections. *Look across the incidents you describe. Can you identify common antecedents, consequences, underlying discourses? (See Chapter 6.)*

Take the Child's Perspective. *Take a moment to reflect on and empathize with the student. How might the child's behavior reflect his or her attempts to meet his or her need to feel competent, autonomous, or connected?*

Clarify Goals. *Take a moment to clarify your goals and your student's goals. How can they be aligned?*

Identify Strategies for the Future. *Identify a tangible strategy, or strategies, you can implement. How could you change the classroom structures, tasks, or your behavior to improve your interactions with this student?*

KEY TERMS

Boundaries/boundary setting: Institutional, intellectual, interpersonal, cultural, or personal barriers teachers put up that allow them to focus on the shared learning goals of their class and protect themselves from burnout.

Compassion fatigue: Feelings of exhaustion and disconnection experienced by teachers when they take on the problems of their students and colleagues.

Composure: Involves engaging in behaviors that move teachers to a state of calm self-control—a place where they can respond to students productively.

Dual relationships: A relationship between a student and a teacher that becomes personal rather than professional; they can lead to positive student impact but can also lead to teacher burnout.

Emotional labor: The feelings of burnout and fatigue teachers feel when they are frequently asked to display emotions that are inconsistent with what they actually feel (i.e., suppressing anger).

Empathy: Considering the feelings of another; it can be used by teachers to connect with uninviting students.

Gentle discipline: Developing a system of private signals that attempt to redirect students when they engage in problem behaviors.

Influence: The degree to which a teacher feels he or she can impact an uninviting student.

Positive intent: Efforts by a teacher to offer student a positive behavioral choice after the student has misbehaved.

Productive reflection: A teacher's efforts to reflect in a focused and systematic manner on the quality of his or her relationship with each of his or her students, particularly students who are uninviting.

Restitution: Attempts to repair a relationship or situation after harm has been done.

Self-composure: Efforts by a teacher to remain nonreactive in the face of strong emotions; it can be used to model positive reactions to students.

References and Further Reading

Ames, C. (1990). Motivation: What teachers need to know. *Teachers College Record, 91*, 409–421.

Anderson, J. D. (2007). Race-conscious educational policies versus a "Color-Blind Constitution": A historical perspective. *American Educational Research Association, 36*(5), 249–257.

Andrzejewski, C. E., & Davis, H. A. (2008). Human contact in the classroom: Negotiation of context in teachers' touch decision-making. *Teaching and Teacher Education, 24*, 779–794.

Arcia, E., Frank, R., Sánchez-LaCay, A., & Fernáindez, M. C. (2000). Teacher understanding of ADHD as reflected in attributions and classroom strategies. *Journal of Attention Disorders, 4*, 91–101.

Aron, A., Aron, E. N., & Smollan, D. (1992). Inclusion of other in the self scale and the structure of interpersonal closeness. *Journal of Personality and Social Psychology, 63*, 596–612.

Aultman, L. P., Williams-Johnson, M. R., & Schutz, P. (2009). Boundary dilemmas in teacher-student relationships: Struggling with "the line." *Teaching and Teacher Education, 25*, 636–646.

Bailey, B. A. (2000). *Conscious discipline: 7 basic skills for brain smart classroom management.* Oviedo, FL: Loving Guidance. [See also http://www.consciousdiscipline.com/]

Baker, J. A. (1999). Teacher-students interaction in urban at-risk classrooms: Differential behavior, relationship quality, and student satisfaction with school. *Elementary School Journal, 100*, 57–70.

Baker, J. A., Grant, S., & Morlock, L. (2008). The teacher-student relationship as a developmental context for children with internalizing or externalizing behavior problems. *School Psychology Quarterly, 23*, 3–15.

Battistich, V., Elias, M. J., & Branden-Muller, L. R. (1992). Two school-based approaches to promoting children's social competence. In G. W. Albee, L. A. Bond, & T. U. Monsey (Eds.), *Improving children's lives: Global perspectives on prevention* (pp. 217–234). Thousand Oaks, CA: Sage.

Battistich, V., & Horn, A. (1997). The relationship between students' sense of their school as a community and their involvement in problem behaviors. *American Journal of Public Health, 87,* 1997–2001.

Battistich, V., Schaps, E., & Wilson, N. (2004). Effects of an elementary school intervention on students' "connectedness" to school and social adjustment during middle school. *Journal of Primary Prevention, 24,* 243–262.

Battistich, V., Watson, M., Solomon, D., Lewis, C., & Schaps, E. (1999). Beyond the three R's: A broader agenda for school reform. *Elementary School Journal, 99*(5), 415–432.

Beaty-O'Ferrall, M., Green, A., & Hanna, F. (2010). Classroom management strategies for difficult students: Promoting change through relationships. *Middle School Journal, 41,* 4–11.

Ben-Ze'ev, A. (2000). *The subtlety of emotions.* Cambridge, MA: MIT Press.

Birch, S. H., & Ladd, G. W. (1997). The teacher-child relationship and children's early school adjustment. *Journal of School Psychology, 35*(1), 61–79.

Blackburn, M. (2005). Talking together for a change: Examining positioning between teachers and queer youth. In J. A. Vadeboncoeur & L. Patel (Eds.), *Re/constructing "the adolescent": Sign, symbol, and body* (pp. 249–270). New York, NY: Peter Lang.

Bondy, E., & Ross, D. (2009). The teacher as warm demander. In M. Scherer (Ed.), *Engaging the whole child: Reflections on best practices in learning, teaching, and leadership* (pp. 55–63). Alexandria, VA: Association for Supervision and Curriculum Development.

Brantlinger, E., & Danforth, S. (2006). Critical theory perspective on social class, race, gender, and classroom management. In C. E. Evertson & C. S. Weinstein (Eds.), *Handbook of classroom management: Research, practice, and contemporary issues* (pp. 157–180). Mahwah, NJ: Lawrence Erlbaum.

Brophy, J. (1981). Teacher praise: A functional analysis. *Review of Educational Research, 51,* 5–32.

Brophy, J. (1988). Educating teachers about managing classrooms and students. *Teaching and Teacher Education, 4,* 1–18.

Brophy, J. (1996). *Teaching problem students*. New York, NY: Guilford Press.

Brophy, J. (1999). Perspectives of classroom management: Yesterday, today, tomorrow. In H. J. Frieberg (Ed.), *Beyond behaviorism: Changing the classroom management paradigm* (pp. 43–56). Boston, MA: Allyn & Bacon.

Brophy, J. (2000). *Motivating students to learn*. New York, NY: Routledge.

Brophy, J. (2006). History of research on classroom management. In C. E. Evertson & C. S. Weinstein (Eds.), *Handbook of classroom management: Research, practice, and contemporary issues* (pp. 17–43). Mahwah, NJ: Lawrence Erlbaum.

Brophy, J., & McCaslin, M. (1992). Teachers' reports of how they perceive and cope with problem students. *Elementary School Journal, 93,* 3–68.

Brown, D. F. (2003). Urban teachers' use of culturally responsive management strategies. *Theory Into Practice, 42,* 277–282.

Brown, D. F. (2004). Urban teachers' professed classroom management strategies: Reflections of culturally responsive teaching. *Urban Education, 39,* 266–289.

Burke, M. D., Ayres, K., & Hagan-Burke, S. (2004). Preventing school-based antisocial behaviors with school-wide positive behavioral support. *Journal of Early and Intensive Behavior Intervention, 1,* 66–74.

Burroughs, N. F. (2007). A reinvestigation of the relationship of teacher nonverbal immediacy and student compliance-resistance with learning. *Communication Education, 56,* 453–475.

Case, C. (1997). African American othermothering in the urban elementary school. *The Urban Review, 29,* 25–39.

Chang, M., & Davis, H. A. (2009). Understanding the role of teacher appraisals in shaping the dynamics of their relationships with students: Deconstructing teachers' judgments of disruptive behavior/students. In P. Schutz & M. Zembylas (Eds.), *Advances in teacher emotion research: The impact on teachers' lives* (pp. 95–127). New York, NY: Springer.

Coie, J. D., & Dodge, K. A. (1988). Multiple sources of data on social behavior and social status in the school: A cross-age comparison. *Child Development, 59,* 815–829.

Connell, J. P., & Wellborn, J. G. (1991). Competence, autonomy, and relatedness: A motivational analysis of self-system processes. In M. R. Gunnar & L. A. Sroufe (Eds.), *Self processes and development: The Minnesota symposia on child psychology* (pp. 43–77). Hillsdale, NJ: Lawrence Erlbaum.

Cornelius-White, J. (2008). Learner-centered student-teacher relationships are effective: A meta-analysis. *Review of Educational Research, 77,* 113–143.

Corno, L., & Snow, R. (1986). Adapting teaching to individual differences among learners. In M. C. Wittrock (Ed.), *Third handbook of research on teaching* (pp. 601–629). New York, NY: Macmillan.

Cowie, H., Smith, P. K., Boulton, M., & Laver, R. (1994). *Cooperation in the multi-ethnic classroom: The impact of cooperative group work on social relationships in middle schools.* London, UK: David Fulton.

Crick, N. R., & Ladd, G. W. (1993). Children's perceptions of their peer experiences: Attributions, loneliness social anxiety, and social avoidance. *Developmental Psychology, 29,* 244–254.

Curran, M. E. (2003). Linguistic diversity and classroom management. *Theory Into Practice, 42,* 334–340.

Daniels, D. H., & Clarkson, P. K. (2010). *A developmental approach to educating young children: Classroom insights from educational psychology series.* Thousand Oaks, CA: Corwin.

Davis, E. A. (2006). Characterizing productive reflection among preservice elementary teachers. *Teaching and Teacher Education, 22,* 281–301.

Davis, H. A. (2001a). *Making the connection: A multi-method case study of relationships between middle school students and teachers.* Dissertation in Educational Psychology, Applied Cognition and Development, Department of Educational Psychology, University of Georgia, Athens, GA.

Davis, H. A. (2001b). The quality and impact of relationships between elementary school students and teachers. *Contemporary Educational Psychology, 26,* 431–453.

Davis, H. A. (2003). Conceptualizing the role and influence of student-teacher relationships on children's social and cognitive development. *Educational Psychologist, 38*(4), 207–234.

Davis, H. A. (2006). Exploring the contexts of relationship quality between middle school students and teachers. *Elementary School Journal, 106,* 193–223.

Davis, H. A. (2008). Development: 3–5. In T. Good (Ed.), *21st century education: A reference handbook* (Vol.1, pp. 82–92). Thousand Oaks, CA: Sage.

Davis, H. A. (2009). Caring teachers. In E. Anderman & L. Anderman (Eds.), *Psychology of classroom learning: An encyclopedia (PCL)* (Vol. 1, pp. 138–141). New York, NY: Macmillan Reference.

Davis, H. A. (in press). Teacher-student relationships. In J. Hattie & E. Anderman (Eds.), *International handbook of student achievement*. New York, NY: Routledge.

Davis, H. A., Chang, M., Andrzejewski, C. E., & Poirier, R. (2010). Examining behavioral, relational, and cognitive engagement in smaller learning communities: A case study of reform in one suburban district. *Journal of Educational Change, 11*, 345–401.

Davis, H. A., Gableman, M., & Wingfield, R. (2011). "She let us be smart:" Low-income African American first grade students' understandings of teacher closeness and influence. *Journal of Classroom Interaction: The structure and function of teacher management and care in classroom settings, 46*, 4–16.

Davis, H. A., & Lease, A. M. (2007). Perceived organizational structure for teacher liking: The role of peers' perceptions of teacher liking in teacher-student relationship quality, motivation, and achievement. *Social Psychology in Education: An International Journal, 10*, 403–427.

Davis, H. A., Shalter-Bruening, P., & Andrzejewski, C. E. (2008, April). *Examining the efficacy of strategy intervention for ninth grade students: Are self-regulated learning strategies a form of social capital?* Paper presented at the annual conference of the American Educational Research Association, New York, NY.

DeAngelis, T. (2009, February). Micro-Aggressions. *American Psychological Association's Monitor on Psychology*, 43–46.

Deci, E. L., & Ryan, R. M. (2000). The "what" and "why" of goal pursuits: Human needs and the self determination of behavior. *Psychological Inquiry, 11*(4), 227–268.

Delpit, L. (1995). The silenced dialogue: Power and pedagogy in educating other people's children. In *Other people's children: Cultural conflict in the classroom* (pp. 21–47). New York, NY: New Press.

DeVries, R., & Zan, B. (1996). A constructivist perspective on the role of the socio-moral atmosphere in promoting children's development. In C. T. Fosnot (Ed.), *Constructivism: Theory, perspectives, and practice* (pp. 103–119). New York, NY: Teachers College Press.

Dover, A. G. (2009). Teaching for social justice and K-12 student outcomes: A conceptual framework and research review. *Equity & Excellence in Education, 42*(4), 506–524.

Doyle, W. (1986). Classroom organization and management. In M.E. Wittrock (Ed.), *Handbook of research on teaching* (3rd ed., pp. 392–431). New York, NY: Macmillan.

Dweck, C. (1996). Implicit theories as organizers of goals and behavior. In P. M. Gollwitzer & J. A. Bargh (Eds.), *The psychology of action: Linking cognition and motivation to behavior* (pp. 60–90). New York, NY: Guilford Press.

Dweck, C. (1999, Spring). Caution: Praise can be dangerous. *American Educator*, 4–9.

Eccles, J. S., Wong, C. A., & Peck, S. C. (2006). Ethnicity as a social context for the development of African-American adolescents. *Journal of School Psychology, 44*, 407–426.

Emmer, E., Evertson, C., & Anderson, L. (1980). Effective classroom management at the beginning of the school year. *Elementary School Journal, 80*, 219–231.

Emmer, E. T., & Gerwels, M. C. (2006). Classroom management in middle and high school classrooms. In C. M. Evertson & C. S. Weinstein (Eds.), *Handbook of classroom management: Research, practice, and contemporary issues* (pp. 407–438). Mahwah, NJ: Lawrence Erlbaum.

Ennis, C. D. (1996). When avoiding confrontation leads to avoiding content: Disruptive students' impact on curriculum. *Journal of Curriculum and Supervision, 11*, 145–162.

Evertson, C., & Emmer, E. (1982). Effective management at the beginning of the school year in junior high classes. *Journal of Educational Psychology, 74*, 485–498.

Figley, C. (1995). Compassion fatigue as secondary traumatic stress disorder: An overview. In C. R. Figley (Ed.), *Compassion fatigue: Secondary traumatic stress disorder in helpers* (pp. 82–101). New York, NY: Brunner Mazel.

Finkelstein, B. (2001). Is adolescence here to stay? Historical perspectives on youth and education. In T. Urday & F. Pajares (Eds.), *Adolescence and education: General issues in the education of adolescents* (Vol. 1, pp. 1–32). Greenwich, CT: Information Age.

Finn, J. D. (1989). Withdrawing from school. *Review of Educational Research, 59*, 117–142.

Finn, J. D. (1993). *School engagement and students at risk*. Washington, DC: National Center for Educational Statistics.

Finn, J. D., & Voelkl, K. E. (1993). School characteristics related to student engagement. *Journal of Negro Education, 62*, 249–268.

Fisher, B. (1998). *Joyful learning in kindergarten*. Westport, CA: Greenwood/Heinemann.

Ford, D. Y., & Grantham, T. C. (2003). Providing access for culturally diverse gifted students: From deficit to dynamic thinking. *Theory Into Practice, 42*, 217–225.

Ford, M. E. (1987). Processes contributing to adolescent social competence. In M. E. Ford & D. H. Ford (Eds.), *Humans as self-constructing living systems: Putting the framework to work* (pp. 199–233). Hillsdale, NJ: Erlbaum.

Ford, M. E. (1992). *Motivating humans: Goals, emotions, and personal agency beliefs.* Newbury Park, CA: Sage.

Ford, M. E. (1996). Motivational opportunities and obstacles associated with social responsibility and caring behavior in school contexts. In J. Juvonen & K. Wentzel (Eds.*), Social motivation: Understanding children's school adjustment* (pp. 126–153). New York, NY: Cambridge University Press.

Ford, M. E., & Nichols, C. W. (1987). A taxonomy of human goals and some possible applications. In M. E. Ford & D. H. Ford (Eds.), *Humans as self-constructing living systems: Putting the framework to work* (pp. 289–311). Hillsdale, NJ: Erlbaum.

Ford, M. E., & Nichols, C. W. (1991). Using goal assessments to identify motivational patterns and facilitate behavioral regulation and achievement. In M. L. Maehr & P. Pintrich (Eds.), *Advances in motivation and achievement: Vol. 7. Goals and self-regulatory processes* (pp. 51–84). Greenwich, CT: JAI Press.

Franke, M. L., Carpenter, T., Fennema, E., Ansell, E., & Behrend, J. (1998). Understanding teachers' self-sustaining generative change in the context of professional development. *Teaching and Teacher Education, 14,* 67–80.

Franke, M. L., Carpenter, T. P., Levi, L., & Fennema, E. (2001). Capturing teachers' generative change: A follow-up study of professional development in mathematics. *American Educational Research Journal, 38,* 653–689.

Frea, W., Crag-Unkefer, L., Odom, S. L., & Johnson, D. (1999). Differential effects of structured social integration and group friendship activities for promoting social interaction with peers. *Journal of Early Intervention, 22*(3), 165–174.

Fredricks, J. A., Blumenfeld, P. C., & Paris, A. H. (2004). School engagement: Potential of the concept, state of the evidence. *Review of Educational Research, 74,* 59–109.

Frey, N. (2011).*The effective teacher's guide: 50 ways to engage students and promote interactive learning.* New York. NY: Guilford Press.

Frieberg, H. J. (1999a). Beyond behaviorism. In H. J. Frieberg (Ed.), *Beyond behaviorism: Changing the classroom management paradigm* (pp. 3–20). Boston, MA: Allyn & Bacon.

Frieberg, H. J. (1999b). Consistency management & cooperative discipline: From tourists to citizens in the classroom. In

H. J. Frieberg (Ed.), *Beyond behaviorism: Changing the classroom management paradigm* (pp. 75–97). Boston, MA: Allyn & Bacon.

Frieberg, H. J., & Stein, T. A. (1999). Measuring, improving, and sustaining healthy learning environments. In H. J. Frieberg (Ed.), *School climate: Measuring, improving, and sustaining healthy learning environments* (pp. 11–29). London, UK: Routledge Falmer.

Frieberg, H. J., Stein, T., & Huang, S. (1995). Effects of a classroom management intervention on student achievement in inner-city elementary schools. *Educational Research and Evaluation: An International Journal on Theory and Practice, 1,* 36–66.

Friedman, I. A. (1995). Student behavior patterns contributing to teacher burnout. *Journal of Educational Research, 88*(5), 281–289.

Frymier, A. B. (1994). A model of immediacy in the classroom. *Communication Quarterly, 42,* 133–144.

Furrer, C., & Skinner, E. (2003). Sense of relatedness as a factor in children's academic engagement and performance. *Journal of Educational Psychology, 95*(1), 148–162.

Gay, G. (2006). Connections between classroom management and culturally responsive teaching. In C. E. Evertson & C. S. Weinstein (Eds.), *Handbook of Classroom Management: Research, Practice, and Contemporary Issues* (pp. 343–370). Mahwah, NJ: Lawrence Erlbaum Associates.

Gillies, R. M. (2007). *Cooperative learning: Integrating theory and practice.* Thousand Oaks, CA: Sage.

Glasser, W. (1977). Ten steps to good discipline. *Today's Education, 66,* 61–63.

Glickman, C., & Tamashiro, Ro. (1980). Classifying teachers' beliefs about discipline. *Educational Leadership, 37*(6), 459–464.

Goldstein, L. S. (1999). The relational zone: The role of caring relationships in the construction of mind. *American Educational Research Journal, 36,* 647–673.

Goodenow, C. (1992, April). *School motivation, engagement, and sense of belonging among urban adolescent students.* Paper presented at the annual meeting of the American Educational Research Associaion, San Francisco, CA.

Goodenow, C. (1993a). Classroom belonging among early adolescent students: Relationships to motivation and achievement. *Journal of Early Adolescence, 13,* 21–43.

Goodenow, C. (1993b). The psychological sense of school membership among adolescents: Scale development and educational correlates. *Psychology in the Schools, 30,* 79–90.

Graham, S. (1992). "Most of the subjects were White and middle class": Trends in published research on African Americans in selected APA journals, 1970–1989. *American Psychologist, 47,* 629–639.

Greene, B. A., Miller, R. B., Crowson, H. M., Duke, B. L., & Akey, K. L. (2004). Predicting high school students' cognitive engagement and achievement: Contributions of classroom perceptions and motivation. *Contemporary Educational Psychology, 29*(4), 462–482.

Greene, R. W., Beszterczey, S. K., Katzenstein, T., Park, K., & Goring, J. (2002). Are students with ADHD more stressful to teach? Patterns of stress in an elementary school sample. *Journal of Emotional and Behavioral Disorders, 10,* 79–89.

Guralnick, J. M. (1999). The nature and meaning of social integration for young children with mild developmental delays in inclusive settings. *Journal of Early Intervention, 22,* 70–86.

Hall, J. A., Rosenthal, R., Archer, D., DiMatteo, M. R., & Rogers, P. L. (2001). Nonverbal skills in the classroom. *Theory Into Practice, 16,* 162–166.

Hargreaves, A. (1998). The emotional practice of teaching. *Teaching and Teacher Education, 14,* 835–854

Hartup, W. W. (1989). Social relationship and their developmental significance. *American Psychologist, 44,* 120–126.

Heck, M. L. (2004). Cultural narratives: Developing a three-dimensional learning community through braided understanding. *Journal of Social Studies Research, 28*(2), 36–46.

Herrenkohl, L. R., & Guerra, M. R. (1998). Participant structures, scientific discourse, and student engagement in fourth grade. *Cognition and Instruction, 16*(4), 431–473.

Hijzen, D., Boekaerts, M., & Vedder, P. (2007). Exploring the links between students' engagement in cooperative learning, their goal preferences and appraisals of instructional conditions in the classroom. *Learning and Instruction, 17*(6), 673–687.

Hochschild, A. R. (1979). Emotion work, feeling rules, and social structure. *American Journal of Sociology, 85,* 551–575.

Hochschild, A. R. (1983). *The managed heart: Commercialization of human feeling.* Berkeley, CA: University of California.

Howard, T. C. (2003). Culturally relevant pedagogy: Ingredients for critical teacher reflection. *Theory Into Practice, 42,* 195–202.

Howes, C., Hamilton, C. F., & Philipsen, L. C. (1998). Stability and continuity of child-caregiver and child-peer relationships. *Child Development, 69,* 418–426.

Hoy, A. W., Davis, H. A., & Pape, S. J. (2006). Teacher knowledge and beliefs. In P. A. Alexander & P. H. Winne (Eds.), *Handbook of educational psychology* (2nd ed., pp. 715–737). Mahwah, NJ: Lawrence Erlbaum.

Hoy, W. K. (2001). The pupil control studies: A historical, theoretical, and empirical analysis. *Journal of Educational Administration, 39,* 424–442.

Irvine, J. J. (1988). An analysis of the problem of disappearing Black educators. *Elementary School Journal, 88,* 503–514.

Irvine, J. J. (1990). *Black students and school failure: Policies, practices, and prescriptions.* New York, NY: Praeger.

Irvine, J. J. (2003). *Educating teachers for diversity: Seeing with a cultural eye.* New York: Teachers College Press.

Irving, J., & Fraser, J. (1998). Warm demanders. *Education Week, 17,* 56.

Jang, H., Reeve, J., & Deci, E. L. (2010). Engaging students in learning activities: It is not autonomy support or structure but autonomy support and structure. *Journal of Educational Psychology, 102*(3), 588–600.

Johnson, D. W., & Johnson, F. P. (2009). *Joining together: Group theory and group skills* (10th ed.). Upper Saddle River, NJ: Pearson.

Johnson, D. W., & Johnson, R. T. (1989). *Cooperation and competition: Theory and research.* Edina, MN: Interaction Book.

Johnson, D. W., & Johnson, R. T. (1998). Cooperative learning and social interdependence theory. In S. R. Tindale & L. Heath (Eds.), *Theory and research on small groups: Social psychological applications to social issues* (Vol. 4, pp. 9–35). New York, NY: Plenum.

Johnson, D.W., & Johnson, R. T. (2003). Student motivation in cooperative groups: Social interdependence theory. In R. M. Gillies & A. F. Ashman (Eds.), *Cooperative learning: The social and intellectual outcomes of learning in groups.* New York, NY: Routledge Falmer.

Johnson, D. W., Johnson, R. T., & Maruyama, G. (1983). Interdependence and interpersonal attraction among heterogeneous and homogeneous individuals: A theoretical formulation and meta-analysis of the research. *Review of Education Research, 53,* 5–54.

Jones, V., & Jones, L. (2007). *Comprehensive classroom management: Creating communities of support and problem solving* (8th ed.). Boston, MA: Allyn & Bacon.

Kessen, W. (1979). The American child and other cultural inventions. *American Psychologist, 34,* 815–820.

Kinderman, T. A. (1993). Natural peer groups as contexts for individual development: The case of children's motivation in school. *Developmental Psychology, 29*, 970–977.

Kleinfeld, J. (1975). Effective teachers of Eskimo and Indian students. *School Review, 83*, 301–344.

Knee, C. R., Patrick, H., & Lonsbary, C. (2003). Implicit theories of relationships: Orientations toward evaluation and cultivation. *Personality and Social Psychology, 7*, 41–55.

Kounin, J. S. (1970). *Discipline and group management in classrooms.* New York, NY: Holt, Rinehart & Winston.

Kurcinka, M. S. (2000). *Kids, parents, and power struggles: Winning for a lifetime.* New York, NY: Harper Collins.

Kurdek, L. A., & Sinclair, R. J. (2000). Psychological, family, and peer predictors of academic outcomes in first- through fifth-grade children. *Journal of Educational Psychology, 92*, 449–457.

Ladd, G. W. (1990). Having friends, keeping friends, making friends, and being liked by peers in the classroom: Predictors of children's early school adjustment? *Child Development, 61*, 1081–1100.

Ladd, G. W., Birch, S. H., & Buhs, E. S. (1999). Children's social and scholastic lives in kindergarten: Related spheres of influence? *Child Development, 70*, 1373–1400.

Ladson-Billings, G. (1997). It doesn't add up: African American students' mathematics achievement. *Journal for Research in Mathematics Education, 28*, 697–708.

Ladson-Billings, G. (2001). *Crossing over to Canaan: The journey of new teachers in diverse classrooms* (pp. 101–122). San Francisco, CA: Jossey-Bass.

Lambert, N. M., & McCombs, B. L. (1998). *How students learn: Reforming schools through learner centered education.* Washington, DC: American Psychological Association.

Lannutti, P. J., & Strauman, E. C. (2006). Classroom communication: The influence of self-disclosure on student evaluations. *Communication Quarterly, 54*, 89–99.

Lareau, A. (1987). Social class differences in family-school relationships: The importance of cultural capital. *Sociology of Education, 60*, 73–85.

Lareau, A., & Horvat, E. M. (1999). Moments of social inclusion and exclusion: Race, class, and cultural capital in family-school relationships. *Sociology of Education, 72*, 37–53.

Lawrence, S., & Tatum, B. D. (1997). Teachers in transition: The impact of antiracist professional development on classroom practice. *Teachers College Record, 99,* 162–178.

Leary, M. R. (2004). Digging deeper: The fundamental nature of "self-conscious" emotions. *Psychological Inquiries, 15,* 129–131.

Lipstein, R., & Renninger, K. A. (2007). Interest for writing: How teachers can make a difference. *English Journal, 96*(4), 79–85.

Lortie, D. C. (2002). *Schoolteacher: A sociological study* (2nd ed). Chicago, IL: University of Chicago Press.

Lotan, R. A. (2006). Managing groupwork in heterogeneous settings. In C. E. Evertson & C. S. Weinstein (Eds.), *Handbook of classroom management: Research, practice, and contemporary issues* (pp. 525–540). Mahwah, NJ: Lawrence Erlbaum.

Maines, B., & Robinson, G. (1992). *Michael's story: The "no blame" approach.* Bristol, UK: Lame Duck.

Manke, M. P. (1997). *Classroom power relations: Understanding student-teacher interaction.* Mahwah, NJ: Lawrence Erlbaum.

Martin, N. K., Yin, Z., & Baldwin, B. (1998, April). *Classroom management training, class size, and graduate study: Do these variables impact teachers' beliefs regarding classroom management style?* Paper presented at the annual meeting of the American Educational Research Association. San Diego, CA. ERIC Document Reproduction Services No. ED 420 671

Marzano, R. J., Marzano, J. S., & Pickering, D. J. (2003). *Classroom management that works: Research-based strategies for every teacher.* Alexandra, VA: ASCD.

McCaslin, M., Bozack, A. R., Napoleon, L., Thomas, A., Vasquez, V., Wayman, V., & Zhang, J. (2006). Self-regulated learning and classroom management: Theory, research and considerations for classroom practice. In C. E. Evertson & C. S. Weinstein (Eds.), *Handbook of classroom management: Research, practice, and contemporary issues* (pp. 223–252). Mahwah, NJ: Lawrence Erlbaum.

McCaslin, M., & Good, T. (1992). Compliant cognition: The misalliance of management and instructional goals in current school reform. *Educational Researcher, 21*(3), 4–17.

McCombs, B. (n.d.). *Developing responsible and autonomous learners: A key to motivating students* [Teacher module]. Retrieved from http://www.apa.org/education/k12/learners.aspx

McMillan, D. W., & Chavis, D. M. (1986). Sense of community: A definition and theory. *Journal of Community Psychology, 14,* 6–23.

Meehan, B. T., Hughes, J., & Cavell, T. A. (2003). Teacher-student relationships as compensatory resources for aggressive children. *Child Development, 74,* 1145–1157.

Metallidou, P., & Viachou, A. (2007). Motivational beliefs, cognitive engagement, and achievement in language and mathematics in elementary school children. *International Journal of Psychology, 42,* 2–15.

Middleton, M. J., & Blumenfeld, P. C. (2000, April). *Types and sources of academic press in middle school science classrooms.* Paper presented at the annual meeting of the American Educational Research Associations, New Orleans.

Middleton, M. J., & Midgley, C. (2002). Beyond motivation: Middle school students' perceptions of press for understanding in math. *Contemporary Educational Psychology 27,* 373–391.

Milner, H. R. (2003). Teacher reflection and race in cultural contexts: History, meaning, and methods in teaching. *Theory Into Practice, 42,* 173–180.

Milner, H. R. (2006). Classroom management in urban settings. In C. E. Evertson & C. S. Weinstein (Eds.), *Handbook of classroom management: Research, practice, and contemporary issues* (pp. 491–522). Mahwah, NJ: Lawrence Erlbaum.

Moje, E. B. (1996). "I teach students, not subjects": Teacher-student relationships as contexts for secondary literacy. *Reading Research Quarterly, 31,* 172–195.

Monroe, C. R., & Obidah, J. E. (2004). The influence of cultural synchronization on a teachers' perceptions of disruption: A case study of an African American middle-school classroom. *Journal of Teacher Education, 5,* 256–268.

Morine-Derschimer, G. (2006). Classroom management and classroom discourse. In C. M. Evertson & C. S. Weinstein (Eds.), *Handbook of classroom management: Research, practice, and contemporary issues* (pp. 127–156). Mahwah, NJ: Lawrence Erlbaum.

Muller, C., Katz, S., & Dance, L. (1999). Investing in teaching and learning. Dynamics of the teacher-student relationship from each perspective. *Urban Education, 34,* 292–337.

Murdock, T. B. (1999). The social context of risk: Status and motivational predictors of alienation in middle school. *Journal of Educational Psychology, 91,* 62–75.

Murdock, T. B., Bolch, M. B., Dent, G., & Wilcox, N. H. (2002). Motivation and African American youth: Exploring assumptions of some contemporary motivation theories. *Research on sociocultural influences on motivation and learning* (Vol. 2, pp. 249–271). Greenwich, CT: Information Age.

Murphy, P. K., Delli, L. A., & Edwards, M. N. (2004). The good teacher and good teaching: Comparing beliefs of second-grade students, preservice teachers, and inservice teachers. *Journal of Experimental Education, 72*, 69–92

Newberry, M. (2010). Identified phases in the building and maintaining of positive teacher–student relationships. *Teaching and Teacher Education, 26*, 1695–1703.

Newberry, M., & Davis, H. A. (2008). The role of elementary teachers' conceptions of closeness to students on their differential behavior in the classroom. *Teaching and Teacher Education, 24*, 1965–1985.

Nie, Y., & Lau, S. (2009). Complementary roles of care and behavioral control in classroom management: The self-determination theory perspective. *Contemporary Educational Psychology, 34*, 185–194.

Noblit, G. (1993). Power and caring. *American Educational Research Journal, 30*, 23–38.

Noddings, N. (1988). An ethic of caring and its implication for instructional arrangements. *American Journal of Education, 96*, 215–230.

Noddings, N. (1995). A morally defensible mission for schools in the 21st century. *Phi Delta Kappan, 76*(5), 365–368.

Oldfather, P., & Dahl, K. (1994). Toward a social constructivist reconceptualization of intrinsic motivation for literacy learning. *Journal of Reading Behavior, 26*, 139–158.

Oldfather, P., West, J., White, J., & Wilmarth, J. (1999). Learning through children's eyes: Social constructivism and the desire to learn. *Psychology in the Classroom: A series in applied educational psychology.* Washington, D.C.: American Psychological Association.

Olweus, D. (1997). Bully/victim problems in school: Knowledge base and an effective intervention project. *Irish Journal of Psychology, 18*, 170–190.

Oplatka, I. (2007). Managing emotions in teaching: Toward an understanding of emotion displays and caring as nonprescribed role elements. *Teachers College Record, 109,* 1374–1400.

Osborne, J. W., & Walker, C. (2006). Stereotype threat, identification with academics, and withdrawal from school: Why the most successful students of colour might be the most likely to withdraw. *Educational Psychology, 26,* 536–577.

Osterman, K. F. (2000). Students' need for belonging in the school community. *Review of Educational Research, 70*(3), 323–367.

Paley, V. (1992). *You can't say you can't play.* Cambridge, MA: Harvard University.

Palinscar, A. S., Anderson, C. W., & David, Y. (1993). Pursuing scientific literacy in the middle grades through collaborative problem solving. *Elementary School Journal, 93,* 643–658.

Palinscar, A. S., & Herrenkohl, L. R. (1999). Designing collaborative contexts: Lessons from three research programs. In A. M. O'Donnel & A. King (Eds.), *Cognitive perspectives on peer learning* (pp. 151–178). Mahwah, NJ: Lawrence Erlbaum.

Palmer, P. J. (1998). *The courage to teach: Exploring the inner landscape of a teacher's life.* San Francisco, CA: Jossey-Bass.

Perry, B. D. (2003). *The cost of caring: Secondary traumatic stress and the impact of working with high-risk children and families.* Child Trauma Academy. Available from www.ChildTraumaAcademy.com

Pianta, R. C. (1999). *Enhancing relationships between children and teachers.* Washington, DC: American Psychological Association.

Pianta, R. C. (2006). Classroom management and relationships between children and teachers: Implications for research and practice. In C. M. Evertson & C. S. Weinstein (Eds.), *Handbook of classroom management: Research, practice, and contemporary issues* (pp. 685–710). Mahwah, NJ: Lawrence Erlbaum.

Pierangelo, R., & Guiliani, G. (2003). *Classroom management techniques for students with ADHD: A step-by-step guide for educators.* Thousand Oaks, CA: Corwin.

Pintrich, P. R. (2003). Motivation and classroom learning. In W. E. Reynolds & G. E. Miller (Eds.), *Handbook of psychology. Vol. 7: Educational psychology* (pp. 103–124). San Francisco, CA: Wiley.

Radley, M., & Figley, C. (2007). The social psychology of compassion. *Clinical Social Work Journal, 35,* 207–214.

Reeve, J. (2006). Teachers as facilitators: What autonomy-supportive teachers do and why their students benefit. *Elementary School Journal, 106*(3), 225–236.

Reeve, J. (2009). Why teachers adopt a controlling motivating style toward students and how they can become more autonomy supportive. *Educational Psychologist, 44*(3), 159–175.

Reeve, J., & Jang, H. (2006). What teachers say and do to support students' autonomy during a learning activity. *Journal of Educational Psychology, 98*(1), 209–218.

Reeve, J., Jang, H., Carrell, D., Jeon, S., & Barch, J. (2004). Enhancing students' engagement by increasing teachers' autonomy support. *Motivation and Emotion, 28*(2), 147–169.

Reid, R. (1999). Attention Deficit Hyperactivity Disorder: Effective methods for the classroom. *Focus on Exceptional Children, 32,* 1. Retrieved from EBSCO host.

Reif, S. F. (1993). *How to reach and teach children with ADD/ADHD: Practical techniques, strategies, and interventions for helping children with attention problems and hyperactivity.* West Nyack, NY: Center for Applied Research in Education.

Render, G. F., Padilla, J. M., & Krank, H. M (1989). Assertive discipline: A critical review and analysis. *Teachers College Record, 90*(4), 607–630.

Richardson, V. (1994). Conducting research on practice. *Educational Researcher, 23*(5), 5–10.

Richmond, P. A., & Padgett, D. L. (2002). Finding the line: Boundary decisions in resident treatment. *Residential Treatment for Children and Youth, 20,* 53–66.

Rigby, K. (1997). Attitudes and beliefs about bullying among Australian school children. *Irish Journal of Psychology, 18,* 202–220.

Rigby, K., & Slee, P. T. (1993). Dimensions of interpersonal relating among Australian school children and their implications for psychological wellbeing. *Journal of Social Psychology, 133*(1), 33–42.

Rimm-Kaufman, S. (n.d.). *Improving students' relationships with teachers to provide essential supports for learning* [Teacher module]. Retrieved from http://www.apa.org/education/k12/relationships.aspx

Rogoff, B. (2003). *The cultural nature of human development.* Oxford, UK: Oxford University.

Rogoff, B., Bartlett, L., & Turkanis, C. G. (2001). Lessons about learning in a community. In B. Rogoff, C. G. Turkanis, & L. Bartlett (Eds.), *Learning together: Children and adults in a school community* (pp. 3–20). New York, NY: Oxford University.

Rogoff, B., Turkanis, C. G., & Bartlett, L. (2001). *Learning together: Children and adults in a school community.* New York, NY: Oxford University.

Rohrkemper, M., & Corno, L. (1988). Success and failure on classroom tasks: Adaptive learning and classroom teaching. *Elementary School Journal, 88,* 296–312.

Roland, E., & Galloway, D. (2002). Classroom influences on bullying. *Educational Research, 44*(3), 299–312.

Rosenthal, R., & Jacobson, L. (1968). *Pygmalion in the classroom: Teacher expectations and pupils' intellectual development.* New York, NY: Holt, Rinehart, & Winston.

Ryan, A. M. (2001). The peer group as a context for the development of young adolescent motivation and achievement. *Child Development, 72,* 1135–1150. doi:10:1111/1467-8624.00338

Ryan, R. M., Connell, J. P., & Deci, E. L. (1985). A motivational analysis of self-determination and self-regulation in education. In C. A. R. Ames (Ed.), *Research on Motivation in Education: Volume 2. The Classroom Milieu.* (pp. 13–51). New York: Academic Press.

Ryan, R. M., & Deci, E. L. (2000). Intrinsic and extrinsic motivations: Classic definitions and new directions. *Contemporary Educational Psychology, 25*(1), 54–67.

Ryan, R. M., Stiller, J. D., & Lynch, J. H. (1994). Representations of relationships to teachers, parents, and friends as predictors of academic motivation and self-esteem. *Journal of Early Adolescence, 14,* 226–249.

Sapon-Shevin, M., Dobbelaere, A., Corrigan, C., Goodman, K., & Mastin, M. (1998). Everyone here can play. *Educational Leadership, 56*(1), 42–45.

Saunders, B., & Chambers, S. M. (1996). A review of the literature on Attention-Deficit Hyperactivity Disorder children: Peer interactions and collaborative learning. *Psychology in the Schools, 33,* 333–340.

Scherer, M. (Ed.). (2009). *Engaging the whole child: Reflections on best practices in learning, teaching, and leadership.* Alexandria, VA: Association for Supervision and Curriculum Development.

Schutz, P. A., & Pekrun, R. (2007). *Emotion in education.* New York, NY: Academic Press.

Sciarra, D., & Seirup, H. (2008). The multidimensionality of school engagement and math achievement among racial groups. *Professional School Counseling, 11,* 218–228.

Scott, T. M., Gagnon, J. C., & Nelson, C. M. (2008). School-wide systems of positive behavior support: A framework for reducing school crime and violence. *Journal of Behavior Analysis of Offender and Victim: Treatment and Prevention, 1,* 259–272.

Shade, B. J., Kelly, C., & Oberg, M. (1997). *Creating culturally responsive classrooms: Psychology in the classroom.* Washington, DC: American Psychological Association.

Shapiro, L. E. (2010). *The ADHD workbook for kids: Helping children gain self-confidence, social skills, and self-control.* Oakland, CA: Instant Help Books.

Sharan, S. (1990). *Cooperative learning: Theory and research.* New York, NY: Praeger.

Skinner, E. A., & Belmont, M. J. (1993). Motivation in the classroom: Reciprocal effects of teacher behavior and student engagement across the school year. *Journal of Educational Psychology, 85,* 571–581.

Slavin, R. E. (1990). *Cooperative learning: Theory, research and practice.* Englewood Cliffs, NJ: Prentice Hall.

Smeh, K., & Fawns, R. (2000). Classroom management of situated group learning: A research study of two teaching strategies. *Research in Science Education, 30*(2), 225–240.

Smith, P. K., Anniadou, K., & Cowie, H. (2003). Interventions to reduce school bullying. *Canadian Journal of Psychiatry, 48,* 591–599.

Solomon, D., Watson, M. S., Delucchi, K. L., Schaps, E., & Battistich, V. (1988). Enhancing children's prosocial behavior in the classroom. *American Educational Research, 25*(4), 527–554.

Soodak, L. C., & McCarthy, M. R. (2006). Classroom management in inclusive settings. In C. M. Evertson & C. S. Weinstein (Eds.), *Handbook of classroom management: Research, practice, and contemporary issues* (pp. 461–489). Mahwah, NJ: Erlbaum.

Stefanou, C. R., Perencevich, K. C., DiCintio, M., & Turner, J. C. (2004). Supporting autonomy in the classroom: Ways teachers encourage student decision making and ownership. *Educational Psychologist, 39,* 99–110.

Stodolsky, S. S., & Grossman, P. L. (1995). The impact of subject matter on curricular activity: An analysis of five academic subject areas. *American Educational Research Journal, 32,* 227–249.

Stodolsky, S. S., & Grossman, P. L. (2000). Changing students, changing teaching. *Teachers College Record, 102,* 125–172.

Straub, E. T., & Davis, H. A. (July, 2006). *Students' and teachers perceptions of connectivity in distance education.* Paper presented as part of the symposia on the *Interpersonal Contexts of Teaching Selves: Where Have We Been and Where Are We Going?* at the Fourth Biennial International SELF Conference, Ann Arbor, MI.

Strickland, D. S., & Asher, C. (1992). Low income African-American children and public schooling. In P. W. Jackson (Ed.), *Handbook of research on curriculum* (pp. 609–625). New York, NY: Macmillan.

Summers, J. J. (2006). Effects of collaborative learning on individual goal orientations from a socio-constructivist perspective. *Elementary School Journal, 106*, 273–290.

Summers, J. J., Beretvas, S. N., Svinicki, M. D., & Gorin, J. S. (2005). Evaluating community and collaborative learning. *Journal of Experimental Education, 73*, 165–188.

Summers, J. J., & Davis, H. A. (2006). Introduction: The interpersonal contexts of teaching, motivation, and learning. *Elementary School Journal: Special Issue on the Interpersonal Contexts of Motivation and Learning, 106*, 189–192.

Summers, J. J., & Svinicki, M. D. (2007). Investigating classroom community in higher education. *Learning and Individual Differences, 17*, 55–67.

Tatum, B. (1997). *Why are all the black kids sitting together in the cafeteria? and other conversations about race.* New York, NY: Basic Books.

Tharpe, R. G., Estrada, P., Dalton, S. S., & Yamauchi, L. A. (2000). *Teaching transformed; achieving excellence, fairness, inclusion and harmony.* Boulder, CO: Westview.

Thompson, R. A. (1990). Emotion and self-regulation. In R. A. Thompson (Ed.), *Socioemotional development.* Nebraska Symposium on Motivation (Vol. 36, pp. 367–467). Lincoln: University of Nebraska.

Thompson, R. A. (1991). Emotional regulation and emotional development. *Educational Psychology Review, 3*, 269–307.

Tingstrom, D. H., Sterling-Turner, H. E., & Wilczynski, S. M. (2006). The good behavior game: 1969–2002. *Behavior Modification, 30*(2), 225–253.

Turner, J. C., Meyer, D., Anderman, E., Midgley, C., Green, M., Kang, Y., & Patrick, H. (2002). The classroom environment and students' reports of avoidance strategies in mathematics: A multimethod study. *Journal of Educational Psychology, 94*, 88–106.

Turner, J. C., Meyer, D. K., Cox, K. C., Logan, C., DiCintio, M., & Thomas, C. T. (1998). Creating contexts for involvement in mathematics. *Journal of Educational Psychology, 90*, 730–745.

Turner, J. C., Meyer, D. K., Midgley, C., & Patrick, H. (2003). Teacher discourse and sixth graders' reported affect and achievement in two high-mastery/high-performance mathematics classrooms. *Elementary School Journal, 103*, 357–382.

U.S. Department of Education (2008, September). *Reducing behavior problems in the elementary school classroom: IES practice guide.* Washington, DC: Institute for Education Sciences, National Center of Education Evaluation and Regional Assistance. Report is available at http://ies.ed.gov/ncee/wwc/publications/practice guides/

Van Gelen, J. (2004). School reform and classwork: Teachers as mediators of social class. *Journal of Educational Change, 5,* 111–139.

Van Ryzin, J. E., Gravely, A. A., & Roset, C. J. (2009). Autonomy, belongingness, and engagement in school as contributors to adolescent psychological well-being. *Journal of Youth and Adolescence, 38,* 1–12.

van Tartwijk, J., den Brok, P., Veldman, I., & Wubbels, T. (2009). Teachers' practical knowledge about classroom management in multicultural classrooms. *Teaching and Teacher Education, 25,* 453–460.

Walker, J. (2008). Looking at teacher practices through the lens of parenting style. *Journal of Experimental Education, 76,* 218–240.

Ware, F. (2006). Warm demander pedagogy: Culturally responsive teaching that supports a culture of achievement for African American students. *Urban Education, 41,* 427–456.

Watkins, D. E., & Wentzel, K. R. (2008). Training boys with ADHD to work collaboratively: Social and learning outcomes. *Contemporary Educational Psychology, 33,* 625–646.

Watson, M., & Battistich, V. (2006a). Building and sustaining caring communities. In C. M. Evertson & C. S. Weinstein (Eds.), *Handbook of classroom management: Research, practice, and contemporary issues* (pp. 253–279). Mahwah, NJ: Erlbaum.

Watson, M., & Battistich, V. (2006b). Building and sustaining learning communities. In C. M. Evertson & C. S. Weinstein (Eds.), *Handbook of classroom management: Research, practice, and contemporary issues* (pp. 253–280). Mahwah, NJ: Lawrence Erlbaum.

Watson, M., & Ecken, L. (2003). *Learning to trust: Transforming difficult elementary classrooms through developmental discipline.* Hoboken, NJ: Jossey-Bass.

Webb, N. M. (1989). Peer interaction and learning in small groups. *International Journal of Educational Research, 13*(1), 21–39.

Weiner, L. (2007). A lethal threat to U.S. teacher education. *Journal of Teacher Education, 58*(4), 274–286.

Weiner, L. (2003). Why is classroom management so vexing to urban teachers? *Theory Into Practice, 42*, 305–312.

Weiner, L. (2000). Research in the 90s: Implications for urban teacher preparation. *Review of Educational Research, 70*(3), 369–406.

Weinstein, C. (1988). Pre-service teachers' expectations about the first year of teaching. *Teaching and Teacher Education, 4*, 31–41.

Weinstein, C. (1998). "I want to be nice, but I have to be mean": Exploring prospective teachers' conceptions of caring and order. *Teaching and Teacher Education, 14*, 153–163.

Weissberg, R. P., Kumpfer, K., & Seligman, M. E. P. (Eds.). (2003). Prevention that works for children and youth: An introduction. *American Psychologist, 58*, 425–432. [Key work for Social and Emotional Learning]

Wells, M. C. (1996). *Literacies lost: When students move from a progressive middle school to a traditional high school.* New York, NY: Teachers College Press.

Wentzel, K. R. (1991a). Social competence at school: Relation between social responsibility and academic achievement. *Review of Educational Research, 61*, 1–24.

Wentzel, K. R. (1991b). Relations between social competence and academic achievement in early adolescence. *Child Development, 62*, 1066–1078.

Wentzel, K. R. (1993). Motivation and achievement in early adolescence: The role of multiple classroom goals. *Journal of Early Adolescence, 13*, 4–20.

Wentzel, K. R. (1994). Relations of social goal pursuit to social acceptance, classroom behavior, and perceived social support. *Journal of Educational Psychology, 86*(2), 173–182.

Wentzel, K. R. (1997). Student motivation in middle school: The role of perceived pedagogical caring. *Journal of Educational Psychology, 89*, 411–419.

Wentzel, K. R. (1998). Social relationships and motivation in middle school: The role of parents, teachers, and peers. *Journal of Educational Psychology, 90*(2), 202–209.

Wentzel, K. R., Barry, C., & Caldwell, K. A. (2004). Friendships in middle school: Influences on motivation and school adjustment. *Journal of Educational Psychology, 96*(2), 195–203. doi:10:1037/0022-0663.96.2.195

Wentzel, K. R., & Caldwell, K. (1997). Friendships, peer acceptance, and group membership: Relations to academic achievement in middle school. *Child Development, 68*, 1198–1209.

Wertsch, J. (1991). *Voices of the mind: A sociocultural approach to mediated action.* Cambridge, MA: Harvard University Press.

Willower, D. J., Eidell, T. L., & Hoy, W. K. (1967). *The school and pupil control ideology.* Penn State Studies Monograph No. 24. University Park: Pennsylvania State University.

Winfield, L. F. (1986). Teacher beliefs toward academically at risk students in inner urban schools. *Urban Review, 18*, 253–268

Wolfgang, C. (1999). *Solving discipline problems: Methods and models for today's teachers.* Boston, MA: Allyn & Bacon.

Woolfolk Hoy, A., Davis, H., & Pape, S. (2006). Teachers' knowledge, beliefs, and thinking. In P. A. Alexander & P. H. Winne (Eds.), *Handbook of educational psychology* (2nd ed., pp. 715–737). Mahwah, NJ: Erlbaum.

Woolfolk Hoy, A., & Weinstein, C. S. (2006). Students' and teachers' perspectives on classroom management. In C. Evertson & C. S. Weinstein (Eds.), *Handbook for classroom management: Research, practice, and contemporary issues* (pp. 181–220). Mahwah, NJ: Erlbaum.

Wubbels, T., Brekelmans, M., den Brok, P., & van Tartwijk, J. (2006). Interpersonal perspective on classroom management in secondary classrooms in the Netherlands. In C. M. Evertson & C. S. Weinstein (Eds.), *Handbook of classroom management: Research, practice, and contemporary issues* (pp. 1161–1191). Mahwah, NJ: Lawrence Erlbaum.

Wubbels, T., Creton, H. A., & Holvast, A. (1988). Undesirable classroom situations: A systems communication perspective. *Interchange, 2*, 25–40.

Wubbels, T., den Brok, P., Veldman, I., van Tartwick, J. (2006). Teacher interpersonal competence for Dutch secondary multicultural classrooms. *Teachers and Teaching: Theory and Practice, 12*, 407–433.

Zentell, S. S., Craig, B. A., & Kuster, D. A. (2011). Social behavior in cooperative groups: Students at risk for ADHD and their peers. *Journal of Educational Research, 104*, 28–41.

Zimmerman, B. J. (2004). Becoming a self-regulated learner: An overview. *Theory Into Practice, 41*(2), 64–70.

Index

Note: Illustrative material is identified by (fig.) or (table).

CORWIN

A SAGE Company

The Corwin logo—a raven striding across an open book—represents the union of courage and learning. Corwin is committed to improving education for all learners by publishing books and other professional development resources for those serving the field of PreK–12 education. By providing practical, hands-on materials, Corwin continues to carry out the promise of its motto: **"Helping Educators Do Their Work Better."**